R-3214-OJJDP

One More Chance

The Pursuit of Promising Intervention Strategies for Chronic Juvenile Offenders

Peter W. Greenwood, Franklin E. Zimring

May 1985

Prepared under a grant from the
Office of Juvenile Justice
and Delinquency Prevention,
U.S. Department of Justice

1700 MAIN STREET
P.O. BOX 2138
SANTA MONICA, CA 90406-2138

SCHOOL OF

CALIFORNIA

PROFESSIONAL

PSYCHOLOGY

LOS ANGELES

PREFACE

This report conveys the principal findings and recommendations of a Rand study funded by the Office of Juvenile Justice and Delinquency Prevention, Department of Justice. The study was designed to identify interventions that hold promise for reducing the criminality of chronic juvenile offenders. A forthcoming Note entitled *The Juvenile Rehabilitation Reader,* edited by Peter Greenwood, contains several essays on related topics that should be of interest to researchers of rehabilitative efforts. The subjects include a historical look at chronic delinquents and their treatment programs; a review of West European programs; legal constraints on intervention; a review of evidence concerning biological contributions to criminality, and the treatments they suggest; school-based interventions; and a cost-benefit model for comparing early intervention with other methods of crime control.

This volume examines the correlates and predictability of chronic delinquency, legal and ethical constraints on state-imposed interventions, and promising methods of prevention or rehabilitation; and it presents an economic comparison of early intervention with selective incapacitation. The findings should be of interest to researchers and practitioners who are attempting to devise methods of reducing the crimes of chronic offenders that are more effective and humane than incarceration.

EXECUTIVE SUMMARY

Two of the most widely accepted findings produced by criminal justice research during the past decade concern the contribution of chronic offenders to this nation's crime problem and the ineffectiveness of rehabilitation programs in reducing subsequent criminality. Chronic offenders are that small proportion of the total offender population who typically begin their criminal activities as juveniles and continue to commit a disproportionate share of crimes throughout their long and active careers. The identification of this group makes them the natural target for any crime control scheme. Reviews of treatment evaluations have not found any particular treatment method that consistently produces recidivism rates lower than would be expected in the absence of the treatment.

If taken at face value, these two concepts suggest that juvenile offenders who exhibit the characteristics and criminal histories that are predictive of chronic offenders should be incarcerated for increasingly long periods of time, as soon as they can be identified. However, there are several troubling aspects to this policy direction. One is that it may not be as effective in reducing crime as is hoped. The extremely high recidivism rates demonstrated by graduates of most traditional juvenile training schools suggests that these offenders will still be committing a large number of crimes, even if they are sentenced to longer terms. Furthermore, the chronic offender research literature shows that criminal behavior can be traced to incompetent or inattentive and inconsistent parenting, combined with inadequate schools and other community resources. Therefore, it is unjust to begin incapacitating juvenile offenders as a crime prevention strategy without making sure that we have tried to alter their delinquent behavior with the best techniques that we know of.

In many instances, we can not now assure ourselves that we have made this effort. Most of the rehabilitation programs tried in the past were either aimed at too broad a range of offenders or too narrowly focused. Many juvenile correctional facilities have ceased making serious attempts to improve the effectiveness of their programs or to measure their results. This report offers a new research model for identifying effective programs and some suggestions for what those programs should contain and where they will be found.

LEGAL AND PRACTICAL LIMITATIONS
ON THE INTERVENTION POWERS
OF JUVENILE COURTS

For most of their history, state juvenile courts had almost absolute power to intervene in the lives of juveniles believed to be in need of supervision or services. It was not even necessary for a child to have committed a criminal act to be found "beyond the control of his parents," and the procedural rules for arriving at such findings were informal at best. This awesome power of the state to intervene was justified on the grounds that it was acting primarily in the child's best interests. The years since the mid-1960s have seen a revolution both in juvenile law as it affects the rights of those accused of delinquency and in the treatment of less serious delinquents.

The procedural revolution was brought about through a series of Supreme Court decisions granting juveniles all of the procedural protections afforded adults, except jury trial and bail. The shift in treatment practices was stimulated by a broad coalition of youth advocacy groups and federal legislation that encouraged local jurisdictions to handle noncriminal truants and runaways through other means than the juvenile court. Because the increase in procedural protection requires the state to prepare juvenile cases just as diligently as if they were adult cases, juvenile courts have had to narrow their focus to those delinquents who are charged with fairly serious criminal acts. Although the pattern of changes across states is highly variable, merely troublesome but noncriminal juvenile behavior is increasingly being turned over to community agencies rather than the juvenile courts, or not being dealt with at all. Once a juvenile has been found to have committed a criminal act, the broad dispositional authority of the juvenile courts to act in the child's best interests remain intact. This situation is very unlike that in criminal courts, which are increasingly being confined to a narrow range of dispositional alternatives determined by the seriousness of the underlying act.

When one looks beyond the juvenile court to identify community agencies that might deal with troublesome but not yet delinquent youth, public schools are the only game in town. Only they command the authority and the resources to act in more than a marginal way. However, it is not clear exactly what they can do. From the standpoint of public law, targeting special groups of students is a risky business. Thirty years of race sensitivity has generated judicial suspicion of selective programs that will disproportionately single out minority students, which targeted programs of delinquency prevention inevitably would. A combination of possible negative stigma attached to a specially targeted program and differential racial effect leaves a targeted program vulnerable to the same constitutional challenges that struck down "tracking" policies in public education. In addition, programs containing a negative stigma may implicate due process requirements for pupil assignment (as is the case in public school discipline), infringe on parental or family liberty, or violate a student's constitutional right to privacy.

CHARACTERISTICS OF CHRONIC OFFENDERS

Although participation in minor delinquent acts is fairly common adolescent behavior, the commission of more serious types of crime is not; chronic participation is rarer yet. Only about 6 percent of all boys raised in an inner city environment will experience five or more arrests before their eighteenth birthday. The more frequently an individual is arrested as a juvenile, the greater the likelihood that he will have a long and active criminal career as an adult.

Five types of factors have been found to be predictive of future offending. The first group are those characteristics of the child's family that indicate poor parenting skills: the father's record of criminal behavior or alcoholism, the mother's history of mental illness, siblings with criminal records, low family income. The second group, biological or physical deficits in the child, indicates impaired neural developments that may impede normal social learning processes: slow autonomic nervous system, abnormal EEG, or the presence of several minor birth defects.

The third category of variables reflects the parenting skills, effort, and attitude of the parents. These include the absence of expressed affection and failure to monitor the child's behavior and to consistently impose appropriate punishments for adverse behavior or rewards for positive behavior. The fourth category of predictor variables are a set of pre-delinquent behaviors that can be identified by teachers or parents. Among younger children these behaviors include being daring or disobedient, stealing, lying, wandering, excessive aggression, and truancy. Among older children, pre-delinquent indicators include heavy drinking or smoking, drug use, promiscuous sex, and fighting. The fifth category is the accumulated record of criminal acts to date. The earlier a child becomes engaged in crime and the more serious and frequent his acts, the more likely he is to continue.

With these five categories of predictor variables, chronic offenders can be identified with about 50 percent accuracy (in attempting to identify the most chronic 20 percent of all youths arrested, the prediction will be correct in one out of two cases) by the time they are about 13 years of age. The advantage of using the family characteristics, family management, biological, and pre-delinquent predictor variables, in addition to the actual delinquent record, is that the system could target its scarce treatment resources on high-risk youths who are most likely to remain chronics unless remedial action is taken, rather than treating all delinquents with similar criminal records alike. Of course the acceptability and effectiveness of such a selective approach would depend on both the characteristics of the treatments to which different types of youths were subjected and the results these treatments produced.

DEALING WITH THE PERCEPTION THAT TREATMENT DOES NOT WORK

The ultimate test of any rehabilitation program is not the technique it uses, or where it takes place, or how hard it tries—the characteristics normally used to describe a model program. The ultimate test is its effect on the criminal behavior of youths after they leave the program: their recidivism rate compared with that of similar youths the program did not treat.

One of the most widely accepted and influential conclusions drawn from criminal justice research over the past two decades is that rehabilitation programs do not work. This conclusion is based on several critical reviews of the treatment evaluation literature that found most experimental programs failed to produce lower recidivism rates and that no intervention method consistently performed better than others or, for that matter, no intervention at all.

The negative conclusion of these reviews has been previously attacked on the grounds that many of the experimental programs were narrowly based or poorly implemented and that many of the evaluations were flawed in design or poorly carried out. In this report we argue that the "nothing works" conclusion is also based on an inappropriate interpretation of the data.

The problem lies in how one defines a treatment method. The traditional evaluation literature groups programs using the same theoretical approach according to some rough taxonomy of intervention strategies. When most of the experimental programs in a given intervention category (say vocational training) do not produce lower recidivism rates, the reviewer concludes that that form of intervention does not work.

This method of evaluation tests the hypothesis that one particular variable, which we happen to call treatment method, dominates all others (type of staff, management, training, etc.) that might be used to define a program. Rejection of this hypothesis simply means that no such dominance exists. Because some individual experimental programs have resulted in lower recidivism rates, even though most of the other programs in the treatment category to which they were assigned did not, other variables than those now used may be important determinants. Our review of currently popular programs was intended to help us determine what those variables might be.

In addition to our criticism of the negative way in which the evaluation literature has been summarized, we have several other reasons why efforts to develop more effective rehabilitation programs should be encouraged. One is the high recidivism rate of most graduates of traditional state training schools. Another is the evidence that a few programs have been effective, at least for a time, in reducing the recidivism rates of particular types of youth. A third is a lack of any more effective alternatives. Although the system can begin resorting to longer incapacitative sentences for the most chronic delinquents, because these youths have extremely high recidivism rates when they are returned to the street, these terms can result in only modest decreases in crime.

The final justification we offer for pursuing more effective intervention techniques has to do with social justice. The youths who are most likely to become chronic offenders are those who have in some sense been failed by their families, their communities, and their schools. It does not seem right that these young men should be consigned to careers of repeated incarceration without our making the maximum effort possible to turn them around. We have identified some programs that are now attempting just that.

PROMISING PROGRAMS FOR CHRONIC JUVENILE OFFENDERS

In the absence of empirical evidence, we must fall back on subjective references to identify the most promising programs operating today. Our reviews of the most accepted theories of how chronic delinquency begins produced the following list of seven essential features for such programs:

1. Provide opportunities for each youth to overcome adversity and experience success, encouraging a positive self-image.

2. Facilitate bonds of affection and mutual respect between juveniles and their guardians, and promote involvement in conventional family and community activities.
3. Provide frequent, timely, and accurate feedback for both positive and negative behavior.
4. Reduce or eliminate negative role models and peer support for negative attitudes or behavior.
5. Require juveniles to recognize and understand thought processes that rationalize negative behavior.
6. Create opportunities for juveniles to discuss family matters and early experiences in a relaxed, nonjudgmental atmosphere.
7. Vary the sequence and amount of exposure to program components to adapt to the needs and capabilities of each participating youth.

Another source of information is the "effective schools" and "safe schools" literature, which attempts to identify and explain the performance of public schools that do much better than expected in improving the achievement levels of poor children or reducing the level of violence within the schools. This body of literature provides another set of important characteristics that focus on management style and attitude rather than program substance. These features include:

1. Continuing instructional leadership and support by school principals.
2. High expectations for student performance and school-wide recognition of success.
3. Frequent monitoring of student progress.
4. Maintenance of an orderly and quiet atmosphere without being oppressive.
5. Collaborative planning and collegial relationships among teachers.
6. Minimizing turnover among the most competent staff.

A third source of subjective evidence is provided by those judges, researchers, and correctional caseworkers who have taken the time to review and compare alternative programs with programs provided by traditional state training schools. The opinions and recommendations of these professionals, combined with concepts derived from the literature, led us to examine the programs described below.

The primary alternatives to traditional training schools that have been developed since the 1970s include outdoor education programs using rugged survival training and other wilderness experience in isolated settings to motivate recalcitrant youths and force them to confront their fears; small, secure intensive treatment units housing no more than 15 violent or acting-out youths who are under continuous supervision and program control; group homes that serve as either entry level placements or reentry facilities for more secure program components; and tracking programs that monitor and supervise youths who reside in the community. Most of these intervention methods have been developed by programs in the private sector.

Two of the more interesting programs that use outdoor education approaches with serious chronic offenders are VisionQuest and Associated Marine Institutes (AMI). Both of these organizations operate multiphased treatment programs in several different sites and neither utilizes any secure facilities to maintain control of their charges. The typical commitment to either program is about one year.

VisionQuest and AMI share several characteristics with many other programs that are being developed by the private sector, and occasionally by a public agency. Each of these programs was founded (and is still run) by dynamic individuals who were discontented with the programs being offered by public agencies. The programs aim at changing behavior, not simply at custody or academic and vocational training. Line level staff and middle management are held closely accountable for their actions and results. None of these programs will tolerate incompetent or inattentive staff. The morale of the staff appears to be quite high and there is a shared sense of purpose, allegiance to the program, and belief that they are having an effect. Program components are in a constant state of evolution in the search for more effective or efficient approaches.

Whether these new wilderness or community program models are any more effective in reducing recidivism rates than the training schools they were designed to replace remains to be seen. Although there are strong differences of opinion about the value of particular techniques or programs, no systematic outcome data have yet been collected that will allow valid comparisons to be made. The principal problem in evaluating new programs is identifying appropriate comparison or control groups. Recidivism data for program participants are meaningless unless they can be compared with recidivism rates of other programs dealing with comparable youths.

PROMISING PROGRAMS FOR ALL KIDS

Although the juvenile court is limited to dealing with juveniles who have exhibited more serious forms of delinquent behavior, the delinquency research literature identifies a much larger pool of younger juveniles, not yet seriously delinquent, but clearly at risk. Are there any acceptable intervention strategies that might be used to reach these youth before they become entangled in the juvenile justice system?

The first principle that must be recognized in considering acceptability is that programs should not be narrowly focused on delinquency prevention alone. Rather, they should address wider social problems— such as drug abuse, school dropout, or unemployment—for which potential delinquents are also at risk. We describe four types of programs that satisfy this requirement and show some promise of reducing later criminal conduct: early education, parent training, effective schools, and voluntary youth service programs.

An early education program, such as Headstart, can help children from high risk families by getting them out of their homes, where they may be neglected or insufficiently stimulated, and bringing them into contact with other children. It helps socialize them to interact with others, prepares them for the discipline of the classroom, and even improves their health by providing them with a good meal. A recent evaluation showed that by the time Headstart children were 19 years old, they were less likely to be arrested and more likely to have completed school than similar children who had not participated in the program.

Parent training as practiced by the Oregon Social Learning Center (OSLC) involves teaching specific techniques for monitoring and changing adverse behavior to the parents of acting-out children. The techniques are based on behavior modification. Because these techniques are fairly simple, the OSLC therapists' most difficult task is to overcome the parents' resistance to putting them into practice. Evaluations have shown that OSLC's techniques are effective in reducing adverse behavior and subsequent delinquency but that the outcome is critically dependent on the skill of the therapists and the cooperation of the parents.

The third type of intervention program that we considered is more effective schools. Many inner cities are plagued by high rates of absenteeism, student dropout, behavior problems and low student achievement—symptoms also characteristic of chronic delinquency. Some evidence suggests that certain school management practices can reduce these problems and possibly also the amount of student delinquency. The evidence is not yet compelling because it is largely subjective and based on comparative case studies.

The fourth type of program we considered is voluntary youth service agencies—for example the California Conservation Corps. The essential features of such programs are that they provide job skills training, work experience and semi-independent living situations in public service programs for young men and women who would probably otherwise be unemployed. Although there is no evidence indicating what effect such programs might have on the recidivism rates of former delinquents, they appear to provide a valuable transition experience for youths who have recently participated in some form of correctional program. There is currently a tendency for the designers of such programs to exclude those with delinquency records.

EARLY INTERVENTION COMPARED WITH SELECTIVE INCAPACITATION AS A CRIME REDUCTION METHOD

Incapacitation and rehabilitation can be viewed as alternative or complementary crime control strategies. By periodically removing him from society throughout the length of his career, incapacitation reduces the number of crimes that an individual chronic offender commits. An effective rehabilitation program would reduce the amount of crime a chronic offender might do either by shortening the length of his career or by reducing the frequency of his criminal acts. The relative efficiency of these two approaches depends on average individual career lengths and rates of offending, the accuracy with which high-rate offenders can be predicted, and the effectiveness of the rehabilitation program in reducing subsequent crime rates.

For any specified distribution of career lengths, individual offense rates, and predictive accuracy, existing models of incapacitation effectiveness can determine the minimum level of effectiveness that a rehabilitation program must achieve and the maximum cost per subject that it can spend to compete with incapacitation as a crime control strategy. The analysis requires four basic steps:

1. Estimating incarceration rates and costs for current sentencing policies;
2. Estimating the increase in offenders incarcerated and expected reduction in crime for particular selective sentencing policies;
3. Determining the minimum level of effectiveness (in reduced recidivism) that a rehabilitation program would have to achieve to produce the same crime reduction achieved in step 2;
4. Estimating the cost savings in reduced incarceration that would be produced by the reduction in recidivism determined in step 3 and, by dividing this figure by the number of predicted chronic delinquents that would have to be treated, determining how much money could be spent on each one.

Based on average sentencing policies and costs nationwide, our analysis suggests that a selective incapacitation policy of doubling prison terms for predicted high-rate offenders would result in a 6 percent increase in the incarcerated population and a 5 percent decrease in total crimes. To produce this same 5 percent reduction in crime, a rehabilitation program for young chronic offenders would have to reduce subsequent individual offense rates by 37 percent. A treatment program that achieved this level of performance would reduce the need for subsequent incarceration by 4 percent, a cost saving of approximately $29,000 per juvenile treated.

POLICY CONCLUSIONS

The principal conclusion of this study is that the development and management of effective rehabilitation programs for chronic juvenile offenders is an extremely demanding and difficult task because of the number of long-standing behavioral, cognitive, and emotional problems that such offenders typically exhibit, and the large degree of uncertainty inherent in any treatment approach. Because of this uncertainty and the high degree of variability with which any treatment method can be implemented, it is extremely unlikely that any one treatment approach will consistently produce results that are better than any other.

To identify and encourage more effective programs, we strongly urge committing agencies to systematically collect and analyze recidivism data for all of the programs they use. We also strongly support the funding of longitudinal studies of high-risk groups, in which subjects are systematically selected to vary their exposure to early-childhood or school-based programs that might be expected to reduce later delinquency. Such programs include prenatal and postnatal care, early-childhood education and daycare, and public schools that are effective in improving academic performance or reducing behavioral problems.

ACKNOWLEDGMENTS

This report does not describe original research but is rather an attempt to draw together and interpret research from several different fields. As such, the authors have been helped tremendously by the contributions and guidance of many colleagues both within and outside of Rand, and the insights provided by many practitioners in the field.

We are thankful to Alfred Regnery, Administrator of the Office of Juvenile Justice and Delinquency Prevention, who funded the study, and to our grant monitors Pamela Swain, Deborah Wysinger, and Richard Sutton for helping to make the administration of our grant as painless as possible. We are also thankful to our Rand colleagues Albert Lipson, Laural Hill, Steven Schlossman, Jacqueline Kimbrough, Peter Rydell, Michele Freier and consultants Marc Miller, Katherine Van Duesen, Gordon Hawkins, and Maria Sanchez for their fine background papers, and Rand colleagues Gene Fisher, Peter Reuter, and Gail Zellman for their helpful reviews of earlier drafts. For their guidance in penetrating their own fields of expertise we are grateful to Gerald Patterson and Pat Chamberlain of the Oregon Social Learning Center, Dale Mann of Columbia Teachers College, Rolf Loeber of the Western Psychiatric Institute and Clinic at the University of Pittsburgh, Sarnoff Mednick of the University of California, Jerome Miller, Director of the National Center on Institutions and Alternatives, and Stanton Samenow of Alexandria, Virginia.

For their assistance in facilitating our entry into the world of current practice, we are grateful to Judges William Gladstone and Seymour Gelber of the Dade County Florida Juvenile Court; Robert Rosof, O. B. Stander, and Nick Millar of the Associated Marine Institutes, Inc.; Dwight Lord of the Jack and Ruth Eckerd Foundation; Judge Terrance Carroll of the King County Juvenile Court, Cathy McBride of the Green Hill School, and John George of the Department of Social and Health Services, all in the State of Washington; Dr. Brendall, principal of John Phillip Sousa Junior High School in the Bronx, and Charles Mitchell, principal of Benjamin Franklin Elementary School in Newark; Michael Smith and Jodi Weisbrod of the Vera Institute of Justice in New York; Kathleen Feely at New York City Department of Juvenile Justice; Ned Murphy, Ned Loughran, Allan Collette, and Betsy Patullo in the Massachusetts Department of Youth Services; Susan Wayne of the Justice Resources Institute; Brian Riley of Massachusetts Halfway Houses, Inc.; Judge Julian Houston of the Roxbury

(Mass.) Juvenile Court; Scott Harscherger, Middlesex County (Mass.) District Attorney; Bob and Claire Burton and Steve Rogers of Vision-Quest in Tucson, Arizona; and Mark Moore and all our fellow participants in the Harvard University Executive Sessions on The Juvenile Justice System.

CONTENTS

FIGURE

TABLES

I. INTRODUCTION

Juvenile courts were founded at the turn of the century in the belief that juvenile offenders should be treated differently from older criminals. The primary focus of these courts was on identifying and eliminating the underlying causes or conditions that were leading the juvenile into delinquency, not on punishing or even determining the specific nature of the criminal acts themselves.

No longer preoccupied with causes of crime or the social history of the delinquent, juvenile courts are now shifting back to standardized punishment to be assigned on the basis of current offense severity and prior proven acts. Juvenile courts are rapidly becoming miniature versions of criminal courts with somewhat reduced powers to punish in return for somewhat reduced due process protections. The jurisdiction of juvenile courts is also being circumscribed by new restrictions excluding delinquents at both ends of the serious spectrum. In many states, juvenile courts now have little if any power over so-called status offenders, who are primarily truants and runaways. For the most serious categories of offenses, many states have enacted mandatory or presumptive waiver statutes that automatically remand older juveniles to the criminal court (Hamperian et al., 1982).

One of the principal shifts in philosophy or perspective that has brought these changes about concerns the nature and effectiveness of rehabilitative programming. Under the original concept of the juvenile court, the purpose of juvenile court hearings was to (1) identify those factors that were causing or contributing to the minor's delinquency, (2) establish a treatment program designed to reduce or eliminate these factors, and (3) monitor its progress. The range of possible treatment programs was as wide as the range of human needs: from a new pair of shoes, so the child could go to school without feeling ashamed, to psychotherapy. Whatever the child needed in the way of treatment, he or she was supposed to get.

We know surprisingly little about the effectiveness or fairness of juvenile courts in their early beginnings; but we know all too well what they became. Under the guise of rehabilitative treatment, many delinquent or merely troublesome youngsters were arbitrarily and summarily placed in detention centers and state training schools that were little better than the prisons they were supposed to avoid. In most states the more extensive forms of "treatment" also involved the most extensive forms of punishment and institutional control. This blending of

1

"treatment," punishment, and control was one of the factors that caused appellate courts to become more concerned about procedural protections in committing a juvenile to "treatment."

The second aspect of rehabilitative treatment that has helped scuttle traditional juvenile court concepts is its apparent futility. Nothing seems to work. Since the 1960s, many carefully designed experimental treatment programs failed to produce any measurable decrease in subsequent arrest rates when the treated youth were compared with similar delinquent youths who had not received the treatment. The principal determinant of a juvenile's future criminality appears to be his record, not what treatment programs he is exposed to. The likelihood of a future arrest begins at about 40 percent for youths with no prior arrests and increases steadily with each arrest until it levels out at about 75 percent for those with five or more. There is no clear evidence that any particular form of intervention will consistently change these probabilities.

The current pattern of juvenile court dispositions reflects these findings. Unless their offenses are unusually serious, delinquents with minor records are given at least one more chance (diverted or placed on summary probation) in hopes that they will straighten out on their own. Those who commit more serious crimes (involving guns or injury to victims) or who have established a lengthy prior record are subject to periods of confinement from 6 to 18 months (Greenwood et al., 1983). The next step is state prison.

The trend toward concentrating the custodial facilities of the juvenile system on chronic offenders has received impetus from the finding that this small group accounts for a disproportionately large share of all serious crime. Although more than 40 percent of all males born in an urban area may experience at least one arrest during their lifetime, less than 10 percent will experience 5 or more arrests. Yet this 10 percent will account for more than 50 percent of all arrests experienced by the total group (Wolfgang et al., 1972). Focusing custodial sentences on chronic offenders can therefore be justified on incapacitation grounds in addition to the factors presented previously.

But is rehabilitation really dead? Interest has been generated by at least three fairly new (or rediscovered) concepts—risk prediction, an alternative paradigm for identifying effective programs, and private sector involvement.

Risk prediction involves an attempt to identify those delinquents who are most likely to engage in sustained criminality. Longitudinal studies have consistently identified several factors, in addition to prior record, that are associated with a predisposition toward delinquency and later criminal activity. These factors include disorganized or ineffective parenting, behavior problems or underachievement in school, and early involvement in delinquent activities. There is still much debate about the practical policy relevance or appropriateness of using these factors for prediction purposes, but they at least raise the possibility of directing prevention and rehabilitative programs more effectively toward high-risk groups.

For an intervention program to be effective as a crime control strategy it must reduce the rate of subsequent criminality of its subjects below what would be expected without the intervention. The conclusion that "nothing works" is based on certain assumptions about what distinguishes one treatment from another, namely that the principal difference among programs is the method of treatment, not the type of staff involved, or the quality of program leadership, or the situation in which it is used, or any of the other factors that might influence program outcomes. The treatment effectiveness literature contains references to programs that have resulted in recidivism rates that were lower than expected. However, other programs that emphasized similar treatment techniques did not achieve lower recidivism rates, so reviewers have concluded that *the treatment techniques* did not work.

Suppose the owner of a professional football team wanted to improve on his team's poor win/loss record. What should he change: his coach, his players, or his plays? Suppose he conducted some studies to find out what difference coaching, players, or plays mean to the effectiveness of a team. If he lists all of the possible characteristics of coaches that he can think of (age, weight, college attended, position, success as a player, etc.) he is unlikely to find characteristics other than their current win/loss records that distinguish the better coaches. Should he then conclude that coaching doesn't matter? If he studied the different formations used by other teams, is he likely to conclude that one particular formation is superior to all the others? Again, not very likely. Otherwise why wouldn't all the other teams have adopted it?

The problem of the football team owner is very similar to that of the public official who wants to establish an effective juvenile offender treatment program. Theories about what methods should be used can only be a guide; they cannot provide clearcut answers. There is no validated theory that tells us how to turn delinquents around, or change other lifestyle patterns, or win football games. The practice of changing people's behavior is as much art as science. Some practitioners will be better than others. Until someone is successful in isolating those factors that invariably lead to more effective treatment programs over and above the obvious ingredients of hard work, consistency, determination, good morale, etc., practitioners will have to continuously monitor program outcomes to know which ones are more effective.

This revised concept of what it takes to build and maintain effective programs has recently been used to explain the success of instructionally effective schools. These schools achieve better than average results raising poor children's academic performance in the face of standard evaluation findings that "nothing works" in education either. A growing body of researchers are now prepared to accept the fact that some programs may be operationally more effective than others, even though these differences in performance cannot be explained by differences in the formal structure or procedures involved in the programs. *Rather, it is the people who run the programs that matter.*

Contract programs have revived interest in the concept of treatment effectiveness. These programs were developed primarily by private contractors in response to demands by some public officials for more diverse, humane, and effective programming. Massachusetts led the way with the abrupt closure of its training schools in 1972. Pennsylvania, Florida, and Utah are now all heavy users of contract programs, and many other states are proceeding along these lines. One of the side effects of this move is a growing cadre of practitioners prepared to argue the merits of different programs, not on the basis of theoretical differences in their approach but because of what they observe in practice.

If either the commitment of juvenile courts to rehabilitation or the capability of the system to deliver on that commitment continues to decline as they have in the past, then the future careers of most chronic juvenile offenders will be fairly predictable. They will become the obvious targets for longer incapacitative sentences. They will spend most of their young adult years locked up in institutions or striving (usually unsuccessfully) to survive and fit into an urban environment that offers few productive roles for individuals with their skills and background.

This report and its companion volume, *The Juvenile Rehabilitation Reader*, are the result of a project funded by the Office of Juvenile Justice and Delinquency Prevention, Department of Justice, which involved more than a dozen participants. The project was designed to determine what avenues, if any, hold out promise for rehabilitating or preventing chronic delinquents. Our research methods included critical reviews of the prediction and treatment literature, observations of programs, interviews with practitioners and former chronic delinquents, statistical modeling, a review of relevant legal statutes and cases, and a historical analysis of how treatment concepts have developed.

This report pulls together and interprets what we believe to be the most current information on programmatic techniques holding promise for preventing chronic delinquency or rehabilitating chronic delinquents once they have begun. The report has been written primarily for those practitioners who control or influence the use of treatment resources and for fellow researchers who are interested in analyzing the effectiveness of alternative treatment methods.

Because our report examines juveniles who are at risk of chronic rather than occasional offending, Section II begins by describing those personal background characteristics that have been shown to be associated with a high risk of chronic delinquency. We then briefly describe and synthesize the principal theories that have been proposed for explaining why juveniles with these characteristics are at risk. Section III reviews the success researchers have had using these variables in predicting chronic delinquency.

In Section IV we step back and review those legal principles that limit courts and other public institutions in the degree to which they can intervene in the lives of predicted or actual delinquents. Section V reviews and critiques the methods that have been used to evaluate the effectiveness of rehabilitation programs and describes several programs about which some practitioners are currently optimistic.

Section VI is devoted to general prevention programs that need not, and according to our legal review, must not, focus on delinquency prevention alone. Not surprisingly, youngsters who are at risk for chronic delinquency are also at risk for poor academic achievement, unemployment, alcoholism, drug dependency, and mental health problems in later life.

One of our primary motivations in undertaking this study was to see whether prevention or rehabilitation programs might offer a viable alternative or supplement to incapacitation (see Greenwood and Abrahamse, 1982) as a means of reducing the large number of crimes attributable to chronic offenders. In Section VII we describe an analysis that compares the costs and effectiveness of these two methods of crime control. Section VIII summarizes our conclusions about the prospects for prevention and rehabilitation programs and recommends how more effective programs might be pursued.

II. PREDICTORS OF CHRONIC
CRIMINAL BEHAVIOR

Although participation in minor delinquent acts is fairly common adolescent behavior, participation in more serious types of offenses is not. Chronic participation is even rarer still. In the Philadelphia cohort study (Wolfgang, Figlio, and Sellin, 1972) 35 percent of the boys born in that city who continued to reside there until their 18th birthday experienced at least one police contact before they turned 18. But only 6 percent of the cohort experienced five or more such contacts. It is these chronics who are most likely to become high-rate adult offenders.

The likelihood of becoming a chronic offender is not equally distributed across the juvenile population. Certain families are much more likely to produce chronic offenders than others. Furthermore, by the time a juvenile has reached about 13 years of age, aspects of his behavior provide further indications of the likelihood that he is headed down the chronic offender path.

To discuss the comparative merits of any intervention programs intelligently, it is necessary to know something about the types of juveniles that these programs must serve. This section provides that information by presenting several leading theories that have been offered to explain how serious delinquency develops. It then describes the specific types of variables that have been found to be associated with high rates of chronic delinquency. It concludes with a discussion of how the apparently competing theories can be reconciled and placed in a perspective that is consistent with the empirical evidence.

THEORIES OF CRIME CAUSATION

Over the years there have been many different theories offered to explain delinquent and criminal behavior (see Empey, 1981, for a review of these theories). Some of the earliest postulated pure genetic or biological bases (Goddard, 1914; Goring, 1913; Lombroso, 1918). Later theories focused on the criminogenic conditions of lower class life (Shaw and McKay, 1931, 1942, 1969; Sutherland and Cressey, 1955; W. Miller, 1958) and the consequences of impaired economic opportunity (A. Cohen, 1955; Cloward and Ohlin, 1960; Quinney, 1974). The theories that are most popular today tend to focus on specific developmental and socializing experiences (Bandura, 1977; Hirschi, 1969; Patterson, 1982) and biological deficits (Mednick and Volavka, 1980) that may impede prosocial development.

This is not the place for a detailed examination of these theories, but some understanding of the basic causal mechanisms thought to be responsible for criminal behavior are necessary to appreciate what prevention or rehabilitation programs must overcome. The six theories we describe here all offer useful insights into how criminal behavior develops.

Each of these theories continues to be discussed and refined in the literature. Each emphasizes a particular set of causal variables or phase in the development of delinquent behavior.

1. Strain Theory (A. Cohen, 1955) holds that although lower class males embrace middle class goals and aspirations, their inability to compete effectively in school and for jobs, because of their inadequate socialization, leads to loss of self-esteem and delinquent drift. One reason lower class youths are inadequately socialized is that their parents tend to be more permissive in controlling their behavior.

2. Control Theory (Hirschi, 1969) holds that humans are naturally antisocial and that a failure of the socialization process (primarily in families) leads to delinquent behavior. This failure causes lack of social competence and achievement and contributes to strain. Socialization is facilitated by bonds between the individual and society. The four elements of these bonds are attachment, commitment, involvement, and belief.

3. Social Learning Theory (Bandura, 1968, 1977) suggests that behavior is acquired and maintained through processes of direct observation, experimentation, and positive and negative reinforcement. Behaviors are copied and then encouraged or discouraged by whether they result in positive or negative reinforcement. Social learning theory provides another explanation of how inadequate or incompetent parenting contributes to later delinquency.

4. Psychoanalytic Theory (Freud, 1963) suggests that parental behavior during the earliest stages of the child's development can lead to apparently aberrant behavior. It emphasizes the continuing effects of stressful incidents or trauma experienced in early childhood on the unconscious mind.

5. Biological Theories (Mednick and Volavka, 1980) describe how various physical endowments or deficits may interfere with normal socialization or learning processes. To some extent, biological and physical endowments are inherited from parents and further influenced by strength of these influences has not yet been determined, but it has been shown that:

- If a natural father has a criminal record, his male offspring, even when adopted at birth, are more likely to have criminal records than similar adoptees whose natural fathers do not have criminal records (Mednick, Gabrielli, and Hutchins, 1984).
- Low birth weight is associated with higher risk of neurological disorders and low academic performance (Harmeling and Jones, 1968).
- Malnutrition during early stages of fetal development produced a 60 percent deficit in the number of brain cells (Winick, 1971).

6. Criminal Personality Theory (Yochelson and Samenow, 1976, 1977) describes the cognitive processes that may contribute to continuing criminal behavior, and is clearly influenced by the preceding theories. Because none of the theories that assign the cause of crime to early socialization processes or physical endowments comes near to explaining all of the variation in criminal behavior, individual cognitive processes must play an important role in the continuation or cessation of criminal activity.

The developmental picture that emerges from the intersection of these theories is consistent with the data presented below. They all help explain how physiological characteristics and parental behavior that are more likely to be found in low income families lead to early antisocial behavior; that in turn, leads to rejection by conventional peers and poor achievements in school, supporting the drift toward more serious delinquent behavior.

THE PREDICTABILITY OF HUMAN BEHAVIOR

For many years scientists, influenced by the discoveries of Newtonian physics, assumed that the universe was completely deterministic. All matter and energy, they thought, obeyed a set of well-defined mechanical laws. The universe was just a big clock. The job of scientists was to deduce the rules by which everything worked. The majority of scientists believed that once these laws were decoded and reduced to precise mathematical equations, the only limitation on their ability to predict future events would be their ability to measure the current state of the universe.

As Einstein and his colleagues were to show, these earlier scientists were wrong. The universe is not a steadily ticking clock but a seething, pulsing conglomeration of infinite complexity. Deterministic predictions about the movement of subatomic particles are not possible because these movements are governed by the laws of probability rather than by fixed mechanical properties.

This brief excursion into hard science is to keep expectations somewhat low concerning our ability to predict human behavior. We cannot predict it well. No one is predestined to criminal behavior, and no one is absolutely immune. The only kinds of statements we can reasonably make are that some types of people are more likely to engage in crime than others. We can identify factors that raise or lower the probability somewhat, but at no time can we be certain about how any one person will behave in the future.

PREDICTOR CATEGORIES

Five types of factors have consistently been found to be correlated with chronic delinquency among urban males.[1] They are, in the chronological order in which they tend to appear, (1) family characteristics, (2) biological or physical endowments, (3) familial experience, (4) predelinquent behavioral flags, and (5) criminal acts. Figure 1 shows how these five categories are interrelated; a sixth category is much more difficult to measure, and its specific effects are largely unknown: the collection of experiences, peer relations, and opportunity structures that either reinforce or discourage whatever delinquent tendencies have developed.

Here we describe the categories of predictor variables and discuss how they are likely to interact. In the next section we show how well these variables can predict chronic delinquency using a variety of statistical approaches. Our primary sources of information concerning these predictive factors are the reviews by Loeber and Dishion (1983) and Farrington (1979) and the longitudinal studies of Farrington (1983) and Robins (1966).

---

[1]The difference in prevalence of criminal acts between boys and girls, as measured by official arrest statistics, is on the order of 4 to 1 (U.S. Department of Justice, 1983). Whether girls display any of the early behavioral warning signs with the same frequency as boys, and if they do why their antisocial behavior is curbed, remain matters of some uncertainty. Participation in serious criminal behavior is predominantly male behavior. Whether the difference in participation rates between the sexes is primarily a reflection of biological temperament, capabilities, or socializing influences is at this point unknown. (1) Some studies show high levels of testosterone associated with higher rates of criminality among boys. (2) Predatory behavior may be a sexual characteristic, as evidenced by the contrasting behavior of male and female homosexuals. Males are primarily promiscuous and predatory, whereas women are not.

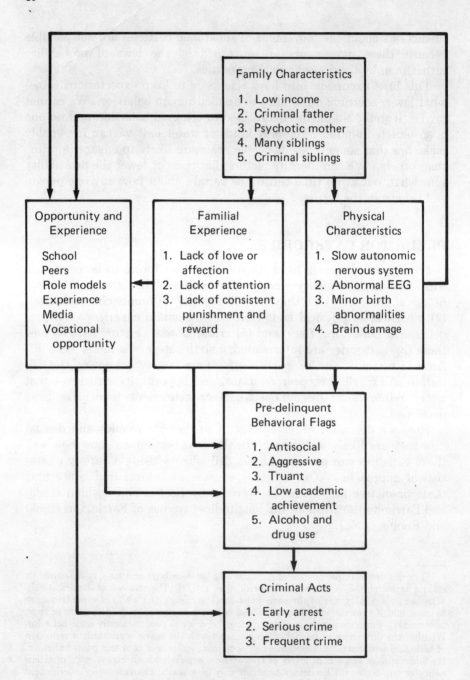

Fig. 1—Predictors of chronic delinquency in urban settings for males

Family Characteristics

Family characteristics that are more likely to produce delinquent boys are low income, father with a history of criminal behavior or alcoholism, mother with a history of mental illness, many siblings, and siblings with criminal records. Rather than causing delinquency directly, these family characteristics can be thought of as leading to or influencing the next two categories, which are more directly associated with delinquency: poor early familial experience and certain biological or physical impairment.

Biological or Physical Impairment

Theories concerning how criminal behavior may be influenced by genetic or physiological characteristics have had a checkered history. In early studies, inappropriate samples and failure to control on other confounding variables produced inflated or otherwise incorrect conclusions about associations between physical features and criminality. More recent work on this subject has produced strong controversy because of the potential for adverse labeling or intervention that physiological predictors imply.

The specific biological and physical characteristics that have been found to be associated with increased rates of delinquency or criminal behavior include (1) slow autonomic nervous system (ANS) as measured by galvanic skin response, (2) abnormal EEGs, (3) presence of several minor birth abnormalities, (4) and various neurological deficits (Freier, 1985). These characteristics are associated with impairment in the brain or nervous system, which in turn may impede the normal social learning process.

Familial Experience

It is generally accepted that the family is the primary socializing agent for the child. It is within the family that a child first learns to control his behavior and get along with other family members. This process of early socialization involves a complex interaction between the behavior of the child's parents or guardian and his own unique biological or physical characteristics. Studies have consistently identified several deficiencies in family functioning and physical characteristics that are associated with increased risk of delinquency. Among familial experiences these include: (1) the absence of expressed love and affection by parents toward the child, (2) failure to monitor the child's behavior, and (3) the failure to impose consistent and appropriate punishments for adverse behavior or rewards for positive behavior.

Our understanding of how these parenting variables affect early childhood behavior has been greatly improved by studies at the Oregon Social Learning Center conducted by Patterson (1982) and his colleagues. They showed how improvements in parenting skills, which can be taught by family therapists, can bring about rapid reductions in some types of adverse behavior and subsequent decreases in delinquency.

Pre-Delinquent Behavioral Flags

The predictive factors in Fig. 1 that we have been discussing up to now represent influences on the child, situations he finds himself in or things that are done to him. As we move on in time, and down the diagram, the predictive factors become things the child does himself. We have labeled the first of these factors Pre-Delinquent Behavioral Flags. Among younger children (ages 6–12) behaviors that are predictive of later delinquency include being daring or disobedient, stealing, lying, wandering, excessive aggression, and truancy (Loeber and Dishion, 1983). For older children, pre-delinquent behavior includes heavy drinking or smoking, drug use, promiscuous sex, and fighting (Osborn and West, 1978; Robins, 1966). Most studies also find that poor verbal skills and low academic achievement are associated with later delinquency.

Criminal Acts

The last set of factors involves explicit criminal acts. The earlier a child becomes involved in crime and the more serious and frequent his criminal behavior, the greater the likelihood of his future criminal behavior. All cohort studies have found a strong correlation between: juvenile and adult arrests; the number of prior arrests and the probability of future arrests; and the age of first arrest and the number of future arrests. In Wolfgang, Figlio and Sellin's (1972) study of boys born in Philadelphia in 1945, the probability that any one boy would be arrested before his eighteenth birthday was 0.35. The probability of a subsequent arrest increased with each prior arrest up to about five, where it leveled off at 0.72.

In Farrington's (1983) study of 411 boys from working class families in London, out of 29 individuals who experienced more than three adult convictions, ten had experienced more than three convictions as juveniles and six had experienced two. Only 2 percent of those with no juvenile convictions experienced more than three convictions as an adult. Most chronic adult offenders will also have been frequent offenders when they were juveniles. Most chronic juvenile offenders will go on to commit crimes as adults. The probability is extremely remote that any individual who was never arrested as a juvenile will become a chronic offender as an adult.

INTEGRATING PREDICTIVE FACTORS AND DELINQUENCY THEORIES

Familial experience and physical characteristics can be thought of as interactive because the child's physical and biological makeup to some extent determines the nature of his behavior and temperament, and his reactions to his parents' behavior. Some children may require more love or attention than others. Some may be slower to learn specific social behavior, thereby pushing the limits of their parents' patience and parenting skills. Some may be hyperactive or easily frustrated, trying their parents' patience in another way. Not all children are equally easy to raise. Not all parents are equally skillful in parenting. Apparently the more difficult the child and the more incompetent, distracted, or inconsistent the parents, the more likely the child is to engage in continuing adverse behavior and later delinquency.

The connection among family characteristics, familial experience and physical characteristics should be obvious. Low income families or those headed by criminal or alcoholic fathers or psychotic mothers are less likely to provide the necessary socializing family experience because of the parents' deficits in skill or preoccupation with their own problems. Large numbers of siblings may detract from the amount of attention that any one child receives, and siblings with criminal records are simply an indication that things have already gone wrong.

Families headed by criminal or alcoholic fathers and psychotic mothers are more likely to be found among low income families; and they are more likely to pass along biological or physical traits to their offspring, either genetically or through prenatal or perinatal influences, that hinder normal socialization. Furthermore, these parents are also more likely to lack the necessary skills, temperament, or dedication necessary for effective parenting.

Patterson (1982) sees the development of delinquency as a two-phase process. In the first phase, the failure of parents to monitor and discipline antisocial behavior results in increased occurrence of problem behavior across home and school settings. The failure of parents to reinforce prosocial behavior is thought to retard the development of social, academic, and possibly work-related skills. The end products of this first phase are high rates of antisocial behavior, low levels of social and academic skills, and a child likely to be rejected by conventional peers.

In the second stage, the lack of social and academic skills increases the likelihood that the child will drift into a deviant peer group, leading in turn to increased delinquent behavior. This drift is exacerbated by the parents' failure to monitor their child's behavior or peers.

Using Patterson's two-stage framework, the first stage is consistent with the control and social learning theories. If we accept the fact that some children may be more difficult to socialize because of their emotional or physiological characteristics, then stage one would also include biological and psychological influences.

Stage two is much more consistent with strain or criminal personality theories. By this period in life the juvenile's deviant behavior creates influences that only beget further deviance unless there is some decided change in his behavior. The only person who can make that change is the delinquent himself. Given his likely background, not just his environment but the habitual patterns of behavior he has fallen into, those changes are difficult to make.

The main point of this section is that the seeds of chronic delinquency are often sown at a very young age. By the time that a child's chronic behavior problems become so disruptive that some remedial action must be taken, their pattern may be extremely well set. If their behavior is to be changed there are a lot of accumulated problems to undo.

III. RISK ASSESSMENT: HOW WELL CAN WE DO?

Most research on criminal careers has been justified in part by the notion that the early prediction of chronic offenders will allow the system to do "something" that it would not be able to do in the absence of this predictive capacity. The "something" that might be done, depending on the philosophy of the researcher and the nature of the predictor variable being used, runs the gamut from early prevention (day care, Headstart, parent training), to heavy investment in treatment programs that focus on specific correlates (drug or alcohol abuse, vocational training), to selective incapacitation during the predicted high risk years. Many of the negative reactions to the concept of risk prediction in the literature are in fact reactions to specific forms of intervention that a predictive capability might seem to justify or permit.

Some argue that the ability to predict future criminality is so fraught with error as to make such predictions practically worthless. Others argue that any criminal justice policies based on predictions of future criminality are inherently unfair, regardless of the data on which they are based, and furthermore that any attempts at prediction or labeling are bound to become counterproductive, self-fulfilling prophecies.

In this field, prediction capability is clearly a two-edged sword. On the one hand it gives us the capacity and rationale for diverting the majority of youth from unnecessarily restrictive placements in the knowledge that their delinquent behavior is unlikely to continue. On the other hand it identifies certain largely underprivileged or neglected youths who, as a group, pose a high risk of future criminal activity to their communities. This section will examine only the feasibility of targeting strategies.

PATTERNS OF ONSET OF CRIMINAL CAREERS

Sources of Data

The best sources of data for examining patterns of onset in criminal careers are those longitudinal studies that have obtained accurate information on both juvenile and adult arrests (Farrington, 1979). The

Cambridge study by Farrington and West (1977) is the best of these, in that it:

1. tracks a large number of subjects over an extended period of time;
2. contains complete juvenile and adult criminal record information; and
3. includes a significant number of serious chronic offenders.

The study covers 411 boys who were aged 8–9 in 1961–1962 and attending six schools in working class areas of London. The boys were contacted every two years up to age 21, and their families were contacted every year till the boys were 15. The study includes all recorded convictions through age 25. Other longitudinal studies containing data on the relationship between juvenile and adult criminality include McCord (1979), who followed 325 boys who had participated in the Cambridge-Somerville project in the late 1930s up through 1975; Robins and Wish's (1977) study of 223 black males born in St. Louis between 1930 and 1934 and followed up to age 18; and Shannon's (1978) study of 1352 youths born in 1942 and 2099 youths born in 1949 in Racine, Wisconsin. The records of both groups were followed up through 1973.

The Connection Between Juvenile and Adult Careers

The Farrington and West data provide the most complete and compelling picture of the connection between juvenile and adult crime. In that study, 70 percent of the sample who were convicted as juveniles (between the ages of 10 and 16) were subsequently convicted as adults (over age 16) by the time they had reached age 24 (Farrington, 1983). The prevalence of convictions for adults who had not sustained any juvenile convictions was only 16 percent, more than a four to one difference. Only 13 out of 411 boys sustained more than three juvenile convictions. Of these 13, 77 percent had four or more convictions as an adult. Only 2 percent of those adults without any juvenile conviction sustained four or more convictions. The small group of boys who were first convicted between ages 10 and 12 averaged six convictions apiece by their 21st birthday (Farrington, 1979).

In the McCord (1979) study, 46 percent of those with juvenile (under age 18) arrests went on to sustain adult arrests compared with only 18 percent for those without juvenile records, a 3 to 1 difference in adult arrest prevalence. In a report on the Racine cohorts published by Shannon (1981), 35 percent of those who committed a felony or major misdemeanor as a juvenile also committed one as an adult compared with a 6 percent prevalence rate for those without much of a juvenile record, a 6 to 1 difference.

ASSESSING THE SIGNIFICANCE OF PREDICTIVE INCREMENTS

One of the problems confronting juvenile justice policymakers is that of resolving conflicting claims about the system's ability to predict future delinquency. Some authors argue that we cannot predict well enough to make any difference in crime rates (Hamparian et al, 1978; Shannon, 1983). Others claim that they can identify a chronic group of offenders that are responsible for a disproportionate share of crime (Wolfgang, Figlio, and Sellin, 1972; Greenwood and Abrahamse, 1982; Farrington, 1983). Are these authors looking at different data or are they reaching different conclusions from the same data? The answer is a little of both.

The accuracy of any predictive model in discriminating among two groups of subjects (delinquent and nondelinquents, or chronic and non-chronics) can be displayed fully in a 2×2 matrix such as that shown in Table 1. This table is taken from Shannon (1983), which questions the value of several recent prediction efforts, including those of Wolfgang

Table 1

PREDICTING ADULT CONVICTION FROM JUVENILE
CONVICTION: CAMBRIDGE STUDY

		Actual Adult Convictions (18–21)		
		No	Yes	
Predicted future criminality based on prior juvenile convictions (age 14–17)	No	(269) .69	(38) .10	.79
	Yes	.08 (32)	.13 (50)	.21
		.77	.23	1.00 (389)

and Farrington. The data are taken from Farrington and West's (1977) analysis of the Cambridge longitudinal data.

The rows represent the two prediction categories—not criminal (no) and criminal (yes), based on juvenile convictions, and the columns represent the actual categories of adult criminality: experiencing (yes) and not experiencing (no) an adult conviction. The decimal figures in each cell show the fraction of cases falling into each category. The numbers at the margins are the sums of the rows or columns. The numbers in parentheses show the actual distribution of the 389 subjects.

The data in Table 1 show that 23 percent of the sample experienced at least one conviction between the ages of 18 and 21, and 21 percent were predicted to sustain convictions on the basis of their juvenile record. The 23 percent convicted include 13 percent who were accurately predicted and 10 percent who were not. Having divided the juvenile population into two groups on the basis of their juvenile records, one with a 62 percent (13/21) chance of being convicted as an adult and the other with 13 percent (10/79) chance, is this a reasonable level of discrimination on which the system might act? Shannon argues it is not.

No one statistic captures all of the possible differences among prediction scales that can appear in such a 2×2 table. Different summary statistics emphasize different aspects of comparison. For instance, in disparaging the predictive value of the Farrington data, Shannon computes what he calls a *Coefficient of Predictability*, which measures the percentage reduction in error over what would arise through chance. On the basis of the data in Table 1, Shannon points out that a prediction that no one would experience an adult conviction would be correct for 77 percent of the cases, the true percentage of those with no convictions. The 23 incorrect predictions would all be false negatives. Using juvenile convictions to predict adult convictions as shown in Table 1 results in 82 percent correct predictions; the 69 percent correctly predicted to have no convictions and the 13 percent correctly predicted to be convicted. Shannon's *Coefficient of Predictability*, which he claims is low, is simply the difference between these two percentage error terms divided by the percentage error under chance:

$$\frac{23 - 18}{23} = .22$$

Shannon's proposed chance method of prediction does not do very well at identifying future offenders in that it predicts none will have convictions. The use of this measure for comparison assumes that all errors in prediction, whether false positives or false negatives, have equal weight, which is usually not the case. For instance, in predicting which defendants are guilty for purposes of conviction, we tolerate many false negatives to keep the percentage of false positives extremely low. However, in screening airport travelers for guns or explosives, we accept a large percentage of false positives to keep the false negatives extremely low. The weight to be given to false positives and false negatives in screening offenders for risk of future criminality will usually fall somewhere between these two extremes and depend on the consequences to the subject and the community of each type of mistake.

An alternative measure of predictive accuracy that takes into account the structure of the decision problem is called *Relative Improvement Over Chance (RIOC)*. RIOC is described in an article by Loeber and Dishion (1983), using the Farrington data in Table 1 in an example as follows:

a. **Compute the random correct (RC)** percentage of predictions that would occur if there were no association between the prediction and outcome variables. For the Farrington data in Table 1 this is the product of the marginals for the two correct cells:

$$(.79 \times .77) + (.23 \times .21) = .66 = RC.$$

b. **Compute the improvement over chance (IOC)**, which is the difference between RC and the fraction predicted correctly (PC) by the prediction scale:

$$PC - RC = .82 - .66 = .16 = IOC.$$

c. **Compute the maximum percentage that could be predicted correctly (MC)** given the true prevalence rate and the *prediction threshold*. For the Farrington data the maximum number of correct predictions would occur if the data in Table 1 were rearranged as shown below:

Adult Convictions
(18–21)

		No	Yes	
Juvenile Convictions	No	77	2	79
	Yes	0	21	21
		77	23	

MC = 98 percent; 2 percent of those with adult records cannot be identified by this particular scale, no matter how accurate it is, because it identifies only 21 percent as positive, and 23 percent actually are. If the prediction threshold were set at the same percentage as the true prevalence, then MC would be 100 percent.

$$Computer\ RIOC = \frac{IOC}{MC - RC}$$

The difference between MC and RC represents the maximum amount that the prediction accuracy can be improved, within the limits of a particular scale. RIOC represents the fraction of the improvement that is achieved.

For the Farrington data in Table 1:

$$RIOC = \frac{.16}{.98 - .66} = .5$$

PREDICTING CHRONICS

Regardless of the statistical measures we use to describe the accuracy of a prediction scale, the true value or utility of the scale can be indicated only by determining how it performs its intended purpose. No one has ever suggested doing anything special to juveniles, to reduce the level of adult crime, on the basis of only one arrest or conviction. A more realistic evaluation of our current predictive capability is provided by Farrington (1983), who attempted to predict the chronic offenders in his sample.

The sample of 411 subjects contains 23 (5.5 percent) who experienced six or more convictions before their 25th birthdays. These "chronics" accounted for half of all the convictions experienced by the sample and presumably at least half of all the crimes. All 23 were convicted as juveniles. Farrington attempted to predict the chronics at age 13 on the basis of data collected earlier and whether they had yet been convicted. The results of these predictions are contained in Table 2.[1]

---

[1]Farrington developed a "Burgess Scale" consisting of seven factors, all equally weighted, to see how accurately the chronics could be identified: (1) rated troublesome by teachers at age 8–10; (2) conduct disorder; (3) acting out; (4) social handicap; (5) criminal parents; (6) poor parental childrearing practices; (7) low I.Q. When he applied this scale to all 411 boys at age 13, 55 boys scored 4 or higher, including 15 of the 23 chronics, 22 others who were convicted at least once, and 18 who were never convicted. Limiting the prediction sample to only those boys who were convicted as youths and using the follow-

The scale predicts accurately in 95 percent (92 + 3) of the cases. It divides the sample into two groups: one (predicted no) consisting of only 2.6 percent chronics, the other (predicted yes) consisting of 55 percent chronics. By focusing on 5.5 percent of the sample (the group predicted to be chronic), or about 20 percent of those with juvenile records, Farrington identified more than half (55 percent) of the chronics. The predicted "yes" group would then presumably be responsible for at least 25 percent of all future crimes attributable to that sample. If some of the false positives include offenders who were not chronic, then the percentage of crime attributable to this group is even higher.

The predictive accuracy achieved by Farrington for juvenile offenders at age 13 is consistent with that found in other studies that have attempted to predict high-rate or chronic offenders (Monahan, Brodsky, and Shah, 1981; Chaiken and Chaiken, 1982) and appears to be near the maximum we can expect. Without these early childhood factors that Farrington used in his prediction scale, attempts to predict chronic offenders would be even less accurate or would have to wait until more of a criminal record had been accumulated.

Table 2

FARRINGTON DATA

		Actual Chronic (6 or more Convictions)		
		No	Yes	
Predicted Chronic	No	92	2.5	94.5
	Yes	2.5	3	5.5
		94.5	5.5	

ing variables in a logistic regression model, Farrington obtained the following results: Of the 17 youths with the highest predicted probability of becoming chronic, 14 were chronics. Lowering the threshold to predict 23 chronics (the same number as there actually were) still identified only 14 true chronics. Of 34 youths first convicted before age 13, 14 became chronics; 13 of these were among the 14 predicted above.

Is the degree of accuracy achieved by Farrington a sufficient basis for treating some juveniles differently from others, even though the number of times they have been convicted may be similar? This is where the concept of bringing just deserts into juvenile court runs headlong into the traditional approach of providing treatment according to needs. If the difference in treatment allows the low-risk juvenile to go free without any punishment or treatment while the high-risk juvenile is placed out of his home or required to participate in an extensive treatment program, then this difference in dispositional severity may be difficult to sustain on the prediction evidence alone. If, however, both youths were required to participate in some type of programming, the predictive factors might be more easily justified in determining the type of program to which each should be assigned. The low-risk youth might be assigned to perform community service. The high-risk youth might be assigned to a more structured and highly supervised program that would attempt to work on some of his behavioral problems or skill deficits through counseling, skill training, or other techniques.

The window of opportunity for dealing with serious delinquent behavior is only about five years in length, extending from the 13th to the 18th birthdate. We cannot afford, nor is it productive in most cases, to make much of a response in the first one or two instances that a juvenile may be arrested. But waiting for chronic offenders to build up a record of many arrests and minor dispositions only compounds the problems that must be dealt with later.

In summary, chronic offenders can usually be identified solely on the basis of their juvenile records. However, this evidence normally does not accumulate until after the youth's 16th birthday. If additional factors describing the youth's school performance and home situation are included, the age at which chronics can be predicted can be moved up several years to possibly the 13th birthdate. This earlier identification might facilitate more productive programming, but it also runs the risk of treating some juveniles who would have desisted on their own. There is little evidence to help us determine the effects of different policies in this area at the current time. The balance we strike must depend on the nature of the interventions imposed and the effects they achieve.

IV. THE LEGAL FRAMEWORK FOR REHABILITATION EFFORTS

In the 1950s, compiling a summary of the legal restraints on delinquency prevention programs and state efforts to rehabilitate clients of the juvenile court was an easy matter. The law was clear, restraints were few, and a broad social consensus supported state power to intervene in the lives of actual and potential juvenile delinquents. The juvenile court, operating under the doctrine of parens patriae, had broad discretionary powers to intervene in the life of a child at risk of harming himself or others. The formal jurisprudence of the juvenile court had changed little during the explosive growth of juvenile justice since the turn of the century. The power of schools and social welfare institutions to intervene in the lives of their juvenile clients was unchallenged.

Many social forces are responsible for complicating the legal framework of juvenile justice since the 1950s. The process of combating official racism implicated the governance of public education in *Brown v. Board of Education* in 1954. Struggles to end racial and gender discrimination involved child- and youth-serving institutions directly and also created a climate for rethinking claims of autonomy and liberty of the young that must be balanced against the public interest in the training, regulation, and discipline of children (Zimring, 1982). Beginning in the 1960s, unquestioning faith in the motives and efficacy of state run programs generally and compulsory programs of rehabilitation in particular was replaced with more skeptical attitudes about the proper limits of the exercise of official power (Allen, 1981). Even as we enter a period of some reaction against this earlier skepticism, we are left with a far more complicated system of checks and balances in the constitutional, statutory, and Common Law framework in which youth-serving institutions function (Zimring, 1982).

What has been called a "revolution in juvenile justice" has produced, over the past 20 years, six important Supreme Court pronouncements on the constitutional status of the juvenile court, a variety of rulings balancing autonomy interests of young persons and their families against educational and social service authorities, and a pattern of legislative adjustments in the jurisdiction, authority, and processes of public youth-serving institutions. By the mid-1970s, an effort to rethink and reform the public law of childhood in the United States produced no fewer than 24 volumes of standards and goals of juvenile justice

(Institute of Judicial Administration and the American Bar Association, 1977; Zimring, 1978).

As the special legal world of childhood and youth has developed and become more complicated, emphasis has shifted from general theories to specific contexts. Broad legal categories, such as the status of minority and the theory of parens patriae, still play an important role in the jurisprudence of youth. But the interplay of these doctrines with different specific settings—such as school, public mental hospitals, the juvenile court—makes generalization across a broad sweep of youth-processing agencies far more hazardous than in earlier times. Accordingly, even this capsule discussion of legal frameworks must separately discuss legal principles involved in the rehabilitation efforts associated with the juvenile court's delinquency jurisdiction and the law's role in delinquency prevention programs situated in the educational system and other public institutions that serve the general youth population (Miller, 1985a).

THE TREATMENT OF DELINQUENCY

It is no accident that constitutional scrutiny has concentrated primarily on the exercise of delinquency jurisdiction in the juvenile court. The analogies between criminal courts and the delinquency jurisdiction of juvenile courts have always been strong, the fit between prisons and training schools close; and the motives of state intervention in the lives of young offenders who commit serious crimes involve a mixture of public protection with concern for the deliquent's welfare.

The specific issues litigated before the United States Supreme Court include procedural protections before an individual can be waived from the jurisdiction of the juvenile court (Kent v. U.S., 1966), counsel and procedural protections in delinquency cases (In Re Gault, 1967), the necessity of proof beyond a reasonable doubt before the status of delinquency can be established (In Re Winship, 1969), the question of whether a jury trial entitlement must be provided in juvenile court delinquency proceedings (McKeiver v. Pennsylvania, 1970), the use of the juvenile court delinquency proceeding as a bar to further prosecution under the double jeopardy clause of the Fifth Amendment (Breed v. Jones, 1975), and the permissibility of prevention detention of juveniles under circumstances that might not be constitutionally permissible for adult defendants processed by criminal courts (Schall v. Martin, 1984).

In reaching conclusions in these cases, the majority of the justices usually denied any competition between the steps required to secure procedural protections and the youth-serving mission and special status of the juvenile court in delinquency cases (Zimring, 1982; Miller, 1985a). Only with respect to jury trial did the court refuse to extend an important procedural entitlement in the criminal courts to the juvenile justice system, and on the express rationale that requiring jury proceedings would threaten the special character of juvenile court delinquency proceedings (McKeiver v. Pennsylvania, 1970).

At the heart of these "procedural" cases was a conception of the *substantive* mission of the juvenile court in delinquency cases. Regarding the court's mission in delinquency cases as solely a miniature version of criminal court processing would necessarily label the juvenile court's substantive mission in these cases as punitive. Exempting the juvenile system from such requirements as jury trial is more consistent with an emphasis on leniency, individualized justice, and youth service.

But questions about the substantive mission of modern juvenile court were only indirectly addressed in the constitutional cases of the early 1970s. More recently, in discussion of the double jeopardy issue (Breed v. Jones, 1975) and in turning back a constitutional attack on preventive detention (Schall v. Martin, 1984), the Supreme Court has turned its attention to a characterization of the particular substantive mission of the juvenile courts in the processing of accused delinquents.

Four principles can be derived from the emerging jurisprudence of delinquency in the United States Supreme Court:

1. Kids are different. Although analogies to criminal court processing are frequently used, the special character of the juvenile offender and the special powers of juvenile courts have never been challenged by majority opinions in the United States Supreme Court. Parens patriae, the doctrine providing broad powers to state government in a quasi-parental role, has not been challenged and was explicitly affirmed in the majority opinion in Schall v. Martin.

2. The interests in liberty of accused delinquents are sufficiently close to those of accused adult offenders that fundamental fairness requires the procedural protections accorded to criminal defendants also be extended to accused delinquents, unless to do so would undermine central elements of the juvenile court's mission.

3. Punishment is an allowable part of the juvenile court's agenda in delinquency cases. The procedural protections extended into the constitutional law of juvenile justice were based in large part on recognition by the justices that punishment is a substantial part of juvenile court policy toward delinquency.

Although informal procedures associated with dealing out punishment were disapproved, the punitive element of delinquency policy has not been seriously challenged.
4. Special powers over the lives of juvenile offenders probably must be based on other than punitive principles.

This last point is stated in more qualified form than the first three because in raising this issue we come to the cutting edge of the Court's jurisprudence. The crucial case is Schall v. Martin, the most recent contribution to the evolving jurisprudence of criminal justice.

The Schall case involved a challenge to secure detention imposed on accused delinquents prior to the adjudication of charges and for the express purpose of protecting both the accused delinquent and the general community from dangerous acts that might otherwise occur. The majority opinion's justification of the substance of the practice was a two-step process. First, the doctrine of parens patriae was interposed to distinguish the case of juvenile detention from criminal court analogies:

> Children by definition are not assumed to have the capacity to take care of themselves. They are assumed to be the subject of the control of the parents and if parental control falters, the state must play its part as parens patriae. . . . In this respect, the juvenile's liberty interests may, in appropriate circumstances, be subordinate to the state's "parens patriae" interest in preserving and promoting the welfare of the child (104 Sup. Ct. at 2410).

The second justifying factor was identification of a legitimate state purpose, other than punishment, for the challenged practice. The majority opinion characterized the conditions of secured detention thusly:

> Children are assigned to separate dorms based on age, size, and behavior. They wear street clothes provided by the institutions and partake in educational and recreational programs and counseling sessions run by trained social workers (104 Sup. Ct. at 2413).

These features lead to the conclusion that the detention practice is restrictive "but is still consistent with the regulatory and parens patriae objectives relied upon by the state."

Using this analysis, we can predict both the decisive issues in and probable result of future constitutional challenges to the substance of juvenile justice. Correctional practices imposed on juveniles but not on adult criminal offenders, terms or conditions of confinement unique to juvenile justice, periods of secure confinement in excess of those imposed on adults for the same behavior, and intervention in the lives of juveniles for conduct that would not generate criminal liability for adults must all be justified under the same parens patriae powers invoked in Schall. The crucial question then becomes whether these practices are "consistent with the regulatory and parens patriae objectives" of juvenile justice.

Apparently, the mixed motives of the sanctioning system do not disqualify practices as long as they serve regulatory as well as punitive ends. Misbehavior in detention facilities may be punished in ways that are consistent with the regulatory ends of parens patriae. Thus, the justification of special sanctioning processes for juveniles will largely be a matter of the labels imposed. And the Schall majority opinion indicates a substantial degree of deference will be accorded to the official motives provided by state agents for the exercise of special power over the lives of juveniles.

Under this test, practices that have achieved widespread acceptance as part of the rehabilitative thrust of juvenile justice are likely to be justified. However, experimental initiatives, programs explicitly based on a punitive or a just deserts rationale, and practices that a constitutional court will label—of its own initiative—punitive are more likely to be regarded as outside the realm of parens patriae because they lack the historical sanction considered important in Schall vs. Martin.

The framework used in Schall v. Martin may be subject to important modifications. The majority opinion's approach does not have explicit precedent in the court's prior decisions involving constitutional limits in the treatment of juvenile delinquency. Moreover, a blanket exemption of practices serving regulatory purposes is controversial when applied to cases in adult or juvenile correctional institutions. This approach is more clearly associated with Mr. Justice Rehnquist, the author of Schall, than with a majority of his brethren.

DELINQUENCY PREVENTION PROGRAMS

While constitutional adjudication was changing juvenile court delinquency processing, a series of economic, legislative, and ideological circumstances were taking the juvenile court largely out of the delinquency prevention business. The ideological shift putting pressure on the juvenile court's delinquency prevention jurisdiction was the decline of the rehabilitative ideal, referred to previously, a climate of opinion that questioned the legitimacy as well as the efficacy of official programs designed to intervene coercively in the lives of children at risk. More skeptical attitudes about compulsory rehabilitation, combined with a new emphasis on "justice models" or desert limits[1] in dealing with young offenders, undermine claims of power over the lives of children because they are at risk of future delinquency. At the same time, increasing rates of arrest for seriously delinquent acts and the need to provide more formal and more expensive procedures for accused delinquents reduce the resources available within courts and correctional settings to deal with pre-delinquents and status offenders.

The combination of ideology and economics is a potent one. The appropriateness of juvenile court jurisdiction over status offenders was challenged in the President's Crime Commission. "Radical nonintervention" became a popular as well as evocative slogan for the system reformers in the early 1970s. Movements toward deinstitutionalization and diversion acquired momentum in juvenile justice system initiatives, in state legislation, and finally in the Juvenile Justice and Delinquency Prevention Act at the federal level in 1974. Even earlier, legislation lowering the stakes in pre-delinquency and status offense cases by creating special rubrics for minors or children in need of supervision became a popular paradigm for strategic withdrawal from compulsory rehabilitation of pre-delinquents in secure residential settings.

With the reduction in flow into the juvenile court of youngsters officially labeled as pre-delinquent or status offenders, court-based or probation-based diversion programs have tended to emphasize the accused delinquents left behind. At the same time, the official justification for juvenile court-based programs involving truants and runaways has been under sustained attack, and support for special residential programs for such offenders after court referral has diminished.

The declining role of the juvenile court in the treatment of children at risk can result in a change in the nature of the programs for this group, a change in the location of the programs, or a combination of both. The relocation of delinquency prevention programs in the general social service network almost invariably is accompanied by a shift from compulsory to voluntary treatment. Drop-in centers, runaway hot-lines, community-based shelter care facilities, and pregnancy counseling all depend on the cooperation of their adolescent subjects when they function independently of juvenile court jurisdiction.

The only alternative to juvenile court for prevention programs that are other than voluntary is the public school. The schools are the

---

[1]A "justice model" of sentencing considers only the seriousness of the current offense and possibly the defendant's prior record. It specifically ignores future risk. In a modified justice model, a desert limit would be the maximum or minimum sentence appropriate for a given offense, regardless of any other sentencing considerations (von Hirsch, 1976).

single youth serving institution that deals with a broad cross-section of adolescents at risk in those jurisdictions where the institutions of juvenile justice have withdrawn from the treatment of status offenses and pre-delinquent behavior. Compulsory education laws, together with the programmatic and disciplinary powers ancillary to the power to compel education, provide an alternative framework for mandatory treatment in areas as diverse as truancy, drug abuse prevention, sex education, and delinquency prevention.

Relocating prevention programs in the public schools is, however, far from an insurance policy against legal complications. At the outset, important distinctions must be drawn, first, between general education programs and those that target and identify a minority of students at special risk, and second, between mandatory prevention programs and those that depend on informed consent of students or parents, or both.

A prevention program aimed at all students is far more likely to be characterized as a permissible educational venture and to survive other legal challenges than a specially targeted program. Deciding that all children at a particular grade level require prevention programs (health education, a sex curriculum, materials on drug abuse, etc.) is well within the pedagogical tradition of the public schools. These programs are frequently upheld, although sometimes with special exemptions for parental veto power on a controversial item.

Targeting special groups of students is, from the standpoint of public law, a risky business. Thirty years of race sensitivity has generated judicial suspicion of selective programs that will disproportionately single out minority students, which targeted programs of delinquency prevention would and should. A combination of possible negative stigma attached to a specially targeted program and differential racial effect leaves a targeted program vulnerable to the same constitutional challenges that have struck down "tracking" policies in public education. In addition, programs containing a negative stigma may implicate due process requirements for pupil assignment (as is the case in public school discipline), infringe on parental or family liberty, and violate a student's constitutional right to privacy (a successful claim in one federal district court drug abuse prevention program).

It is thus probable rather than possible that a program capable of conveying negative stigma that is both targeted at a special population at risk within the public school and mandatory in its terms could not withstand constitutional attack. Such programs could, however, be rehabilitated either by requiring effective parental consent to specially targeted programs or limiting school-based preventive treatment to programs suitable for the entire public school population. Requiring parental consent is expensive and risks losing elements of the school population most profoundly at risk, but it also generates the kind of pressure to make programs attractive that guards against the most glaring examples of punishment in the name of treatment. Restricting programs to those designed for the entire school population diminishes the range of treatment options available and appears inefficient where only a small, indentifiable proportion of a school population is at risk. But this strategy has the important advantage of normalizing a prevention program so that it seems an authentic part of the public educational experience.

It is both prudent and probable that public school-based programs will evolve as school-wide adjuncts to the general educational experience rather than specially labeled and targeted attempts to identify high risk groups. Those delinquency prevention programs most likely to survive legal challenge will not be called delinquency prevention.

V. PROMISING APPROACHES TO THE REHABILITATION OF CHRONIC JUVENILE OFFENDERS

The preceding sections have set the stage for our discussion of programs designed to change criminal behavior. We have shown how the juvenile court is limited by legal and practical considerations to focusing on those youths between 13 and 17 years of age who have demonstrated a sustained commitment to criminal activity or have committed a very serious criminal act. Less serious offenders will be diverted or never brought to court. The most serious and older offenders are being sent on to criminal court.

We have shown that the chronic juvenile offenders with whom the courts must contend typically exhibit a combination of social, biological, and academic deficits that can be traced back to their parents' childrearing practices and their early social environment. By the time these juveniles are brought before the court, these deficits have usually produced patterns of cognitive and social development that are completely at odds with the society in which they must learn to live.

The development of these delinquent patterns is not an inexorable process, conditioned on earlier antecedents, but is highly variable. Most children who experience only one or two of these early deficits will eventually outgrow them. Only a few will progress from early antisocial behavior to serious criminal acts. Those who are most likely to persist on this deviant path can be identified at approximately age 13 with about 50 percent accuracy, using predictor variables that reflect their criminal record to date, their behavior and achievement in school, the childrearing practices to which they were exposed, and other characteristics of their family environment.

In this section we will challenge the misconception that "nothing works" and discuss common characteristics of programs that are thought to be effective.

THE FINDING THAT NOTHING WORKS

One of the most widely accepted and influential findings to come out of criminal justice research during the past two decades has been the conclusion that rehabilitative programs do not work. The reports that got the most attention were those by Martinson (1974) and Lipton, Martinson, and Wilks (1975). But several preceding reports (Bailey.

1966; Adams, 1975) and several that came after (Sechrest, White, and Brown, 1979; Martin, Sechrest, and Redner, 1981) all came to the same conclusion:

> With few and isolated experiences, the rehabilitative efforts that have been reported so far have had no appreciable effect on recidivism. (Martinson, 1974.)

> Within the limits noted below, the Panel concludes that Martinson and his associates were essentially correct. There is no body of evidence for any treatment or intervention with criminal offenders that can be relied upon to produce a decrease in recidivism. Where there are suggestions they are just that—suggestions. They prove to be elusive, not replicable, not quite statistically significant, working now only with one group, then only with another. (Sechrest, White and Brown, 1979, p. 31.)

No wonder that enthusiasm for rehabilitative efforts has declined. Is there any reason other than blind faith to keep looking for effective rehabilitative programs? This section is based on the presumption that there is.

Overreliance on punishment or incapacitation are not c013curealls either. Both are expensive. Both result in large prison populations consisting largely of underprivileged and minority young men. And neither, by itself, can have more than a modest effect on crime rates because most punished offenders are quickly returned to the streets (Greenwood and Abrahamse, 1982).

The correctional evaluation literature is not all that great. The evidence is nowhere near compelling enough to warrant scuttling the entire concept. If we were to concede that treatment programs had no beneficial effects, this concession would be disastrous to juvenile justice programs. Rehabilitative considerations would no longer be valid criteria for placement decisions; punishment and incapacitation would become the principal objectives of sentencing as they are the adult system today. The mission of those who work in juvenile programs would shift from that of change agent or facilitator to custodian and guard. The current high rate of recidivism for juveniles committed to institutional care would guarantee a continuing large supply of career criminals for the adult system to deal with (Greenwood et al., 1983).

As long as there is a federal agency concerned with juvenile delinquency, or juvenile justice, one of its primary concerns must be to continue looking for more effective methods of reducing persistent criminal behavior among the young. This section is intended to help OJJDP perform that role.

There are several reasons why the reviewers of the evaluation literature we quoted above came to their discouraging conclusions. One reason they all cited was the low quality of most of the evaluation studies
they had to work with. Many had inadequate research designs for
measuring the success of experimental programs compared with the
traditional programs they were designed to replace. Most failed to
measure or describe the extent to which the experimental program was
actually implemented, or the intensity of the treatment received by
individual youths. Another reason for their negative conclusions was
that many of the programs described in the literature appeared to be
simplistic. However, the primary reason was not because of the evidence they found but how they chose to interpret it.

The conclusion that "treatment does not work" is based on a particular classification or typology of programs that is theory based. Programs are classified according to what are thought to be their primary
method of treatment. Group counseling is different from vocational
training, which is different in turn from behavior modification, even
though the amount of time devoted to these activities may account for
less than 5 percent of the participating offender's time. When
researchers say that none of these treatment methods work what they
mean is that the programs they have studied that fall within that particular treatment category did not consistently produce results better
than other types of treatments (the controls), even through one or two
may have. In other words, treatment or intervention methods are said
not to work unless they consistently produce superior results, no
matter how they are applied or with what they are compared. This
may be an unrealistic test for them to pass. It is akin to arbitrarily
focusing on one particular characteristic of business organizations, such
as their organizational form, personnel practices, or marketing scheme,
and attempting to determine whether any one particular approach is
consistently better than all the others observed. When all the results
were in, one would be hard pressed to convince business executives
that organization, personnel, and marketing plans had no effect on
their results, no matter what the analysis showed.

This method of evaluation turns out to be a test of the hypothesis
that one particular variable, which we happen to call treatment
method, dominates all of the others (types of staff, training, management skills, screening and selection of participants, etc.) that might be
used to define a program. Rejection of this hypothesis simply means
that no such dominance exists. Variables other than those we now use
to define treatment method must also be important in determining outcomes.

The public official who wants to establish an effective juvenile offender treatment program is in exactly the same situation as any business executive who wants to start a new and presumably profitable business. Theories about rehabilitation or making money from business tend to be rather general. To do better than average one must have a certain amount of luck or skill in finding the appropriate combination of management, staff, and operating concepts to produce the desired results.

The development of this skill involves both art and science. Science alone does not produce profitable business or investment methods, nor does it produce foolproof strategies for changing human behavior. The practitioner's dedication, skill, and intuition are also important.

EVIDENCE THAT SOME THINGS DO WORK

The ultimate test of any rehabilitation program is not what technique it uses, or where it takes place, or how hard it tries, or how well people like it—the characteristics that are normally used to describe a "model" program. The ultimate test is its effect on youths after they leave the program—primarily, its effects on their criminal behavior. This may seem an obvious point, but it is ignored more often than it is recognized in the treatment literature. The model programs proposed in the literature are not usually supported by evidence that they lead to lower recidivism rates. Correctional agencies seldom collect the kinds of data that can show whether their current expenditures on testing, diagnosis, classification, and programming lead to lower recidivism rates.

There are several different kinds of evidence suggesting that rehabilitative efforts may not be as consistently unproductive as the current wisdom holds. One source of evidence is those exceptional cases in the body of evaluative studies from which the "nothing works" conclusions are drawn. For instance Lipton, Martinson, and Wilks (1975) reported:

> The failure rate for all boys participating in the Outward Bound School was lower (20 percent) than the expected rate for delinquents in the same age category institutionalized in Massachusetts (35 percent). (p. 251.)

> But the recidivism rate of all the treated boys (in a program of individual psychotherapy within the Boy's Industrial School in Ohio) was significantly lower than the recidivism rate for the entire institutional population. (p. 208.)

The results obtained during a three-to-five year follow-up clearly indicate that the experimental subjects (provided with sociopsychologically oriented supportive counseling combined with comprehensive welfare measures) recidivated in significantly smaller proportions (41 versus 58 percent). (p. 173.)

There is evidence that vocationally oriented training programs for youthful offenders both in institutions and in the community are associated with lower rates of recidivism than standard institutional care. (p. 523.)

In general, individual psychotherapy is more likely to be effective when it is enthusiastically administered to youthful (16 to 20) amenable offenders by interested and concerned therapists with a pragmatic orientation. (p. 525.)

Hawkins and Zimring (1985) suggest that between 1925 and 1939 the English Borstals achieved an exceptionally low rate of recidivism for their youthful charges. A second source of optimism is provided by those judges, correctional caseworkers, and researchers (McKenzie, 1981; Woods, 1982; Armstrong and Altschuler, 1982) who are beginning to identify programs, largely in the private sector, that they perceive to be more effective than traditional training schools in reducing recidivism rates. Occasionally, for example in Florida, this perception is backed by comparative data on recidivism rates, but there is nothing as rigorous as a controlled experiment.

A third source of evidence is provided by recent findings concerning the effectiveness of public schools in improving the academic achievement of children from lower income families. As is currently the case with rehabilitation, during the 1970s education researchers concluded that schools "didn't matter," that no particular instructional techniques could be found that were consistently effective in improving the performance of poor children. Academic performance was thought to be determined primarily by the background characteristics of children and not by the academic programs to which they were exposed or the performance of their school (Coleman et al., 1966; Jencks, 1972; Averch et al., 1972). As is also the case with rehabilitation this pessimistic conclusion was based on a large number of evaluative studies that failed to find any consistent "treatment" effects, as treatments were then being defined; namely particular instructional packages, methods, or classroom management techniques.

A few education researchers believed that the accuracy of the "nothing matters" conclusion was challenged by the existence of some "instructionally effective" schools in which poor children showed much larger gains in academic achievement than would be predicted from their background characteristics. On further study these schools were found to exhibit characteristics that set them apart from their less effective peers (Weber, 1971; Rutter et al., 1979; Edmonds and Frederikson, 1978):[1]

- Continuing instructional leadership and support for teachers from principals.
- High expectations for student performance.
- The development of an integrated curriculum that emphasizes academic skills.
- Frequent monitoring of student progress.
- An orderly and quiet but not oppressive atmosphere.
- Maximization of time on academic activities.
- Collaborative planning and collegial relationships among teachers.
- School-wide staff development and recognition of academic success.
- Techniques for minimizing turnover among the most competent staff.

Although these characteristics may seem obvious or commonplace, they are also apparently the meat-and-potatoes issues on which effective instructional programs are based, and they are frequently neglected ingredients in inner-city schools. Whether or not these particular ingredients turn out to be important determinants of school effectiveness, the point is that there appear to be many more important ingredients than the curriculum design and classroom organization variables that have dominated the education evaluation literature for the past several years (Goodlad, 1984). We take up these findings again in Section VI to show how they relate to delinquency prevention.

As people have begun to examine the characteristics of delinquency treatment programs with reputations for effectiveness, they are finding characteristics similar to those that distinguish effective schools.

In addition to this meager, but we believe encouraging, evidence we must rely on our own perceptions. Based on our review of the literature and on our own observations and interviews with delinquent youths, we are well aware of the social and emotional deficits from which many of these youths suffer. In retrospect it becomes clear that many of the experimental programs developed and tested during the past two decades failed to address the full array of problems confronting these youths in a realistic manner. In many instances the

---

[1]The evidence in support of the "instructionally effective schools" notion is still rather thin and subject to varying interpretations. See Ralph and Fennessey (1983) for a critique of the literature.

treatment programs were too narrowly focused or too brief in duration. There are good reasons why many of these programs failed and therefore good reasons to believe that not all future programs must fail.

The remainder of this section involves our attempt to synthesize our own perceptions of promising approaches with those of others in this field and in the somewhat similar field of education. We cannot back these perceptions up with tangible proof. That can only come from carefully controlled evaluations in which candidate youths are randomly assigned among experimental and comparison (control) programs. The evidence of past evaluations in the rehabilitation and educational fields indicates that the findings from such evaluations are not likely to identify specific methods or strategies of treatment that are consistently superior. Rather they will identify specific programs that are currently effective and possibly suggest some characteristics of these programs that appear to contribute to their success.[2] Although such findings will not provide policymakers with a sure-fire strategy for improving rehabilitative effectiveness, they will be a vast improvement over the pessimistic and defensive attitudes that now enshroud most treatment endeavors.

THEORETICAL INSIGHTS INTO WHAT A REHABILITATION PROGRAM SHOULD ACCOMPLISH

In Section II we described several prominent theories that have been advanced to explain the onset and development of delinquent behavior. In this section we go back to those theories to see what they suggest about how delinquency might be reduced.

For instance, *strain theory* suggests that delinquents have a negative self-image and are pessimistic about their chances of success at conventional activities. Therefore treatment programs might attempt to build a positive self-image and optimistic life view by creating situations in which the delinquent can achieve success. *Control theory* would suggest assisting the delinquent in creating stronger bonds of respect and affection with those in a guardian or mentor position and involvement in conventional community activities. *Social learning theory* provides the rationale for behavior modification techniques,

---

[2]To show that a particular treatment method is consistently superior to other methods it must be faithfully replicated and evaluated against appropriate control groups in a variety of settings. One of the reasons that the replicated programs may not be as good as the original is that good treatment staff typically like to develop their own programs rather than adopt somebody else's (Berman and McLaughlin, 1978).

token economies, and other strategies for creating an environment in which a youth receives frequent and accurate feedback concerning the quality of his behavior. In fact, two other theories, *cultural deviance* (Shaw and McKay, 1969; W. Miller, 1958) and *differential association* (Sutherland and Cressey, 1955) support the use of behavior modification techniques to create positive behavior among delinquents during periods of confinement or close association. *Cultural deviance theory* suggests that delinquents are simply conforming to an alternative social norm, for which they receive support from their peers. *Differential association theory* also holds that tendencies toward delinquent behavior are reinforced by association with delinquent peers or role models. Therefore, one aspect of rehabilitation programming should involve attempting to reduce peer approval or examples of antisocial behavior.

The theory of the *criminal personality* and the treatment methods developed by Yochelson and Samenow (1977) suggests that offenders need to recognize and confront the inappropriate thought patterns that lead to and help rationalize their criminal behavior. *Psychoanalytic theory* suggests that offenders be given opportunities and encouraged to recall and analyze early interactions and relations with parents to come to understand their current feelings better. Theories of *biological predisposition* suggest that the rehabilitation approach that is attempted be individualized to account for the differences that appear to exist among youths in ability to learn from punishment,[3] temperament, physical and mental capacity, etc. Because all of an individual's physiological deficits may not be known, biological theory also supports the concept that treatment approaches should be highly experimental in searching out an approach that is appropriate for each particular youth.

To summarize, in order to deal with the variety of causal factors suggested by the most widely accepted criminologic theories, rehabilitation programs for chronic serious offenders will be successful to the extent that they:

1. Provide opportunities for success and development of positive self-image.
2. Facilitate the development of bonds of affection and respect between juveniles and their guardians and involve them in conventional activities.

---

[3]To control negative behavior, virtually all treatment programs use various punishments ranging from two-minute "time outs" to loss of privileges, to extra duties, isolation, physical exercises, etc.

3. Provide frequent and accurate feedback for both positive and negative behavior.
4. Reduce or eliminate negative role models and peer support for negative attitudes or behavior.
5. Require delinquents to recognize and reflect on inappropriate thought processes that led to negative behavior.
6. Create opportunities for juveniles to discuss early family experiences with appropriate staff.
7. Vary the sequence and exposure to program components to adapt to the needs of each individual youth.

Given these seven principles, some government agency (such as OJJDP) might design and evaluate programs that would test their relative effectiveness. In fact, this kind of theory testing and development is the approach recommended by the second National Academy of Sciences Panel on Rehabilitation (Martin, Sechrest, and Redner, 1981). The problem is that this kind of top-down program development ignores the other important ingredients to program success that observers have recognized in most exemplary education or criminal justice programs—the quality of the personnel involved. Research on effective knowledge utilization (Ellickson et al., 1983) and program development (Berman and McLaughlin, 1978) has shown that effective programs must be developed from the bottom up by those who will operate them. It is all right for the federal government to disseminate the kind of principles described above, but program development must remain a local endeavor. Theoretical principles must be adapted to local customs, capabilities, and needs. The kinds of people who are needed to develop and run such programs cannot be recruited unless they have an opportunity to participate in the program design. A long line of failed experiments has demonstrated that federally designed experimental programs are seldom implemented as their design is intended.[4] Fortunately there are some programs now operating that have operationalized many, if not all, of these theoretical principles.[5]

---

[4]OJJDP's recent Violent Juvenile Offender initiative is a good example. Half of the test sites dropped out of the program and the remainder had trouble maintaining the treatment model and acquiring the appropriate number and type of youth.

[5]It is not only in education and correctional research that top-down program development is under fire. The cover story, "The New Breed of Strategic Planner," in the September 17, 1984 issue of *Business Week* describes the demise of the corporate strategic planning staff in favor of planning by line managers.

WHAT'S WRONG WITH TRAINING SCHOOLS?

The typical placement in most states for chronic juvenile delinquents or those who have committed crimes of violence are training schools or reformatories holding anywhere from 100 to 1000 youths. Lip service is given to rehabilitation purposes, but the real function of these institutions is custody and control. Even though most of the youths attend compulsory academic and vocational classes, the atmosphere within these institutions is very much that of a prison. The hardened offenders are just doing time. The principal influence on the inmates comes from their peers and not the staff. Collaboration with the staff runs against the inmate code. The more aggressive inmates exploit those who are weak. In this atmosphere, violence, intimidation, and sexual exploitation thrive (Bartollas, Miller, and Dinitz, 1976; Feld, 1977). The biggest challenge for a new inmate is to "make it" in the mainstream and not have to go P.C. (protective custody).

Most reformatories fail to reform. To the best of our knowledge they make no appreciable reduction in the very high recidivism rates, on the order to 70 to 80 percent, that are expected for chronic offenders. The best we can say about such institutions is that they seem to have evolved so as to minimize the supervisory demands placed on the custodial staff in maintaining order and control and have routinized those activities that pass as treatment (Greenwood et al., 1983).

ALTERNATIVES TO TRAINING SCHOOLS

The primary alternatives to state training schools that have been developed lately include outdoor education programs that use wilderness challenges as a means of encouraging youths to learn useful skills and confront their fears; small secure units housing no more than 15 violent or acting-out youths; group homes that serve as either an entry level placement or as reentry facilities for youths who are returning to their community from more restrictive settings; and tracking programs in which community case workers supervise and monitor only one or two youths in their own community.

Almost all of the experimentation and development of these models has been undertaken by vendors from the private sector, rather than by public correctional agencies. In Massachusetts and Pennsylvania, the state juvenile correctional agency has contracted with private vendors to develop specific programs. In California and Florida, the development of these programs was instigated by entrepreneurs in the private sector who then sold their programs to juvenile court judges as an alternative to committing youths to the state correctional program. The remainder of this section will describe four models of outdoor education programs and the organizations that run them. We will also discuss a number of issues that are raised by the heavy involvement of the private sector in operating these programs.

Outdoor Education

Camping or wilderness adventure has usually played a peripheral role in juvenile rehabilitation programs. In the 1930s, the Chicago Area Project developed a summer camping component as part of their delinquency prevention efforts (Schlossman and Sedlak, 1983). Many states rotated selected wards from the state training schools through forestry camps where they worked in fire crews or at maintaining trails. The difference with these newer programs is that the outdoor education component has now assumed a central role. Four well-established and respected programs using these concepts are Vision-Quest, Associated Marine Institutes, the Eckerd Foundation, and Homeward Bound. We have picked these four programs as illustrations because they are prominent in states we have studied and several of them are controversial. Many more use similar techniques.

VisionQuest, a for-profit contractor with headquarters in Tucson, Arizona, is probably the largest program of its type, with annual commitments in excess of 500 delinquent youths. VisionQuest typically takes youths committed directly by juvenile courts in Pennsylvania, California, and several other states. The length of stay is usually between one year and eighteen months.

To enter the program, each candidate youth must agree to (1) abstain from drugs and sex during his commitment, (2) not run away, and (3) complete at least two impact programs, which can include residence in a wilderness camp, cross-country travel on a wagon train, or voyaging on a sailing vessel. In addition to its impact programs, VisionQuest conducts counseling sessions with other family members while a youth is in the program and operates several group homes that facilitate reentry into the community. While they are on the wagon train or in wilderness camp, each youth is assigned to a small group (tepee) of about eight other youths and two junior staff. Each wagon train or wilderness camp consists of about 30 to 45 youths and a similar number of staff. Junior staff members sleep in the tepees with the juveniles and are off duty two days in every seven.

In addition to the wagon trains and OceanQuest programs, Vision-Quest is also known for its confrontational style. Committed youths are not allowed to slide by and just "do time." Rather, an individual

program is worked out to ensure that each youth is challenged intellec-
tually, physically, and emotionally. When juveniles do not perform up
to expectations or begin to "act out," they are "confronted" by one or
more senior staff members in an attempt to get them to deal with
whatever issues underlie the poor behavior.

Confrontations are an ongoing part of any VisionQuest activities.
Some critics take exception to VisionQuest's direct confrontational
style, which sometimes results in the staff having to physically restrain
an overwrought youth.[6] This restraint is accomplished only by personal
means, without the aid of any mechanical devices. Other critics fault
VisionQuest for being willing to take the serious delinquents out in the
wilderness without better security.

Associated Marine Institutes is the parent agency for a group of
non-profit programs (Institutes) located in Florida that use various
marine projects as a means of motivating and challenging delinquent
youths. Most of AMI's programs are nonresidential, picking up participating youths in the morning and returning them home in the evening,
five days a week. During a typical stay of six months in the program, a
participating youth will attend remedial classes, learn SCUBA diving
and related safety procedures, study marine biology, and participate in
some constructive work project, such as refurbishing an old boat or
growing ground cover for some commercial site.

AMI also operates a long term residential program at Fisheating
Creek in south-central Florida. In this program, boys committed by
the Dade County Juvenile Court spend six months to a year in an isolated work camp. During the first phase their living conditions are
extremely primitive and their working conditions are rather hard (dig-
ging out stumps to clear an airstrip). Graduation to Phase 2 earns participants the right to sleep in airconditioned quarters and have better
work assignments. The last two phases of the program are spent in
one of the nonresidential Institutes near their home.

One of the distinctive characteristics of non-profit AMI is its heavy
reliance on the capitalist spirit. Employee performance is periodically
assessed by computerized measures (such as G.E.D.s obtained, program
completion rate, or subsequent recidivism rate) applied to all of the
youths. End of the year staff bonuses, based on these performance
measures, can exceed 10 percent of regular salary. Committed youths
can also earn money by participating in various work projects, such as
clearing brush, that AMI has contracted to undertake.

---

[6]The criticism is more than academic. San Diego probation officers have actually
filed child abuse reports against VisionQuest staff for some of their confrontations.
None of these charges has been sustained to date.

Another unique characteristic of AMI is the local Board of Trustees that is established to oversee the activities of each separate Institute. Trustees include those with either political or financial power in their community. Trustee activities can include fund raising, review of program changes, and review of the performance and compensation of Institute staff.

The Eckerd Foundation is another non-profit wilderness program operating primarily in Florida. Eckerd wilderness camps accept acting-out and emotionally disturbed children who are somewhat younger and less serious than those handled by VisionQuest or AMI. The Eckerd camp program is a highly structured effort to use nature and wilderness experiences to motivate academic and social learning. In the midst of a wilderness setting, the youth lives in a small, ongoing, self-sufficient group facilitated by committed participating staff. The program is client-centered with mutually agreed upon participation from youths and their families.

The fourth wilderness program with something like a national reputation is operated by the Department of Youth Services (DYS) in Massachusetts. Homeward Bound utilizes the Outward Bound 26-day format to teach delinquent boys the basics of wilderness travel and survival. The 350 slots a year are allocated proportionately among the Department's various geographical regions. Boys arrive in groups of seven or eight at the beginning of each week. The three staff members who plan and supervise the activities of that particular group will work and live with the boys continuously throughout their 26-day stay.

Each of these four programs is the result of a key individual's vision and determination. Each reflects its founder's unique skills and perspective.

VisionQuest was founded more than ten years ago by Robert Burton and Steven Rogers, two individuals who had grown disillusioned with their work in the Las Vegas juvenile detention unit. The current VisionQuest format has evolved through trial and error but is also based heavily on Burton's experiences as a VISTA worker with the Plains Indians. VisionQuest's organization and ceremonial practices draw heavily on this Indian heritage. The program also reflects the strong family orientation of its founders. The program prefers to hire husband and wife teams who will serve in the field together. Most activities are treated as family events, and participating youths are treated as family members. In response to questions about how he can get his staff members to work such long and continuous hours, Burton's standard reply is that "VisionQuest is not a job, but a lifestyle" to which some are willing to commit. In accepting a promotion to senior staff level, VisionQuest staff make a personal commitment to stay with the program for at least four more years.

AMI was founded by Robert Rosof, a contractor/venture capitalist, after taking a few delinquent boys out on his boat. AMI more than any of the other programs appears to reflect a kind of tough-minded, no-nonsense business approach to the handling of juvenile delinquents. Treatment emphasizes the acquisition of vocational and academic skills more than emotional development. VisionQuest is more interested in getting youths to admit and confront those emotional or family-related problems that led them into crime.

The Eckerd Foundation is the creation of Jack Eckerd, a business and political figure in Florida whose wealth derives from a chain of drug stores carrying his family name. The rehabilitation of juvenile delinquents represents a second career for Eckerd, who now devotes full time to this effort. When he decided to start a juvenile treatment program he had his staff review the experiences of other programs to determine what approaches had proven most promising. Widerness camping was the answer, based on a similar program operated by the Salesman Club of Dallas.

Even the DYS program has similar roots. Before he started Homeward Bound, Alan Collette, the founder and current director, had worked at the Lyman School, DYS's largest secure facility. At his own request he was transferred to a small forestry program being operated by the department out on Cape Cod. About a dozen boys were involved in cleaning toilets in the park and picking up trash. Collette began to look around for a more demanding and effective program concept.

He arranged to be sent by DYS through one of the Outward Bound programs that were then just starting to proliferate. His own personal experiences in the program, and those of his colleagues, encouraged him to develop a similar program for the kids coming through his forestry camp. When Jerry Miller took over DYS and began to move youths out of institutions, Homeward Bound was asked to expand. The program has now survived at least three DYS commissioners and is still going strong. Alan Collette has become one of the more prolific trainers of Outward Bound instructors as his experienced staff members continuously move on to more lucrative positions.

COMMON INGREDIENTS

Each of these programs has its own localized following. Very few people have had the opportunity to visit and compare several of these programs against one another, and few jurisdictions commit their youths to more than one. There is no systematic research effort currently focusing on these programs,[7] and they are virtually unknown among academic criminologists. In a sense these programs represent a grass roots movement, each one building on its own unique capabilities and responding to needs in its area. Yet, to the perceptive visitor who can see behind the program specific terms and activities, it is surprising how much these programs have in common.

Staff

The most striking ingredient that these programs share is their exceptional staff. They all utilize a high ratio of staff to youths approaching one to one.[8] The staff represent a heterogeneous mix of skills and temperament. Many are highly experienced in specific outdoor skills such as mountaineering, boating, or handling livestock. Few are graduates of traditional social work programs. In each program there is a clear sense of common purpose, shared beliefs, high morale, pride, and sense of individual efficacy among the senior staff. These people believe that they are having a positive effect on the kids they deal with.

Turnover among the junior staff tends to be quite high. It is extremely difficult for a young person to know whether he or she will be able to tolerate the long and demanding hours and low pay that go with this type of work, Many opt out themselves. Others are weeded out because they do not meet the stringent requirements of the programs. All junior staff are on a probationary status in which they are carefully supervised and continually tested by the senior staff. Life in these programs for the junior staff is at least as rigorous as it is for the youths.

VisionQuest and Eckerd both accept and integrate girls into all of their programs, and both have a high proportion of female staff. AMI has several girls and female staff in its local programs but none in the

---

[7]The Office of Juvenile Justice and Delinquency Prevention solicited proposals for an Evaluation of Private-sector Programs for Chronic Offenders in 1984. Awards to approximately four programs will be made in early 1985.

[8]To keep their costs comparable to public agencies, all of these programs pay their junior staff much less than they would get as civil servants. They supposedly make up for it in a more pleasant and challenging work environment. The wilderness programs also do not invest in expensive secure facilities or the services to maintain them.

residential program at Fisheating Creek as of 1984. Homeward Bound found that it cannot handle coed groups in a 26-day program and does not seem to attract female staff.

The final characteristic of the staff that must be observed is that they are endlessly cheerful, positive, hard working, friendly, affectionate, and slow to anger. They know from experience that their own personal safety and that of the youths depend on everyone pulling his weight. They are the kind of people that most of us would trust our own kids with.

Program

All of the programs involve increasingly severe physical challenges. All use nature as what could be considered the primary reinforcing agent to a devotee of behavior modification. Activities are organized in such a way that teamwork and cooperation are required. The whole group, staff and youth, invariably suffers when somebody screws up or slacks off. Group peer pressure is strongly oriented toward cooperative behavior.

This type of program places a high premium on specific skill development. When the whole group is going to rappel down the face of a vertical wall, everybody has to know how to handle a rope. If 70 mules and horses are going to get bedded down for the night, and then out on the road again at 8:00 the next morning, the youths who are handling livestock better know their business. A kid from the inner city who is going to help break mustangs better pay attention when he is being shown how to do it.

Among these four programs, VisionQuest and Homeward Bound are the most physically oriented. Almost all 26 days of the Homeward Bound program are devoted to developing the skills required for specific wilderness or physical challenges. VisionQuest intersperses its physical activities with more routine travel, work, and educational programs. AMI's Fisheating Creek program devotes less time and effort to the Outward Bound type of structured physical activities, relying more on the demands of group work projects and vocational skill development. Eckerd, which deals with the youngest age range, is also the less blatantly physical, and more oriented toward nature education. Both AMI and Eckerd are hampered somewhat in the complexity of the programs they can mount by the fact that Florida pays less than half the per diem that Massachusetts, California, and Pennsylvania pay to maintain their youths in these programs—$30 per day rather than $82 to $100+. This is clearly one reason why VisionQuest and Homeward

Bound participants use a wide variety of outdoor equipment while AMI and Eckerd participants have to make do with much less.

In all of these programs the cooperative behavior that is developed in daily activities is reinforced by the group living conditions. In most of the programs staff members live with the youths during the intensive parts of the program. Junior staff members sleep in the same tents or cabins with the youths. They all eat together and share the same food. Entertainment is whatever the group can come up with. Campfire songs and storytelling are frequent, but the ubiquitous television sets and weight lifting equipment that are the primary ingredients of reform school dormitory life are totally absent.

Finally, in contrast to the apparent groupiness of these endeavors, each youngster's program is as individualized as possible. Each of the programs requires its staff to keep fairly detailed records on each youth's progress and problems. Each youth moves through the various phases of the program at his or her own rate. Each one develops his own special relationships with compatible staff members.

Leadership

One of the consistent findings of educational researchers has been that the only characteristic distinguishing effective programs is charismatic leadership. In some sense these rehabilitation programs bear out that finding. They were all founded, and are still run by, individuals most people would consider charismatic.

However, the ingredients of charisma in this particular context are becoming better understood. Each of these programs was established by someone who decided to try something different on his own. They were all mavericks according to conventional wisdom. Each of them has maintained an experimental/developmental attitude toward their programs that remains as dynamic today as it was earlier, when each of them was working with only 8 to 10 youths. They are continuously seeking new ideas. They are constantly modifying their program format. They all are deeply involved in the day to day activities of their program as the occasion requires.

One of the primary characteristics that has been found to distinguish instructionally effective schools is the role of the principal. Effective principals devote a substantial part of their time to monitoring and improving the skills of their teachers. Each individual who runs one of these programs performs a comparable role. Each one is respected by senior staff for practical skills and experience. In each program, staff training and supervision are continuous efforts. In fact, given the close living arrangements that these programs require, socializing and personal development become almost indistinguishable.

Common Problems or Issues

All of these programs to some extent face a common set of administrative problems and conceptual issues. One issue is staff recruitment. Where do you find the kind of people these programs require: People who are willing to work for $900 a month, 24 hours a day, 5 days a week? After you have trained them, how do you keep them from moving on to more lucrative positions? The consensus is that you look for people from rural areas or small towns "who still know how to work."

Case Continuity

Most public correctional systems have frequent interruptions in the continuity of treatment as a youth moves through the system. If he runs away from a group home and is placed in an institution, the institution will generally be run by a completely new organization and set of people. Similarly upon release, his parole will be supervised by a new caseworker who had nothing to do with his institutional stay. Because the job of rehabilitation involves surfacing information about the individual and establishing bonds, these breaks in the continuity of accountability and contact are thought by some to be counterproductive.

All three of the private sector programs have tried to overcome this problem. All of them develop contacts with the youths' parents at the time they are being considered for entry into the program; they maintain that contact during the residential phase and after the youth has returned home. As far as the youth is concerned, he perceives that he is dealing with a single organization with a common set of goals and a consistent perception of his problem from the time he is accepted until he is completely discharged. For instance, in VisionQuest's San Diego program, the husband and wife team who interviewed the youths before they are accepted also run group sessions for the parents while the youths are in the program; they also are available for counseling or just listening after the youths return. Because almost all serious juvenile offenders come from chaotic home situations, this continuity of programming and accountability across the residential, community, and post-program phases of the programs is essential. It also provides the program operators with a better opportunity to observe the effects of their program on youths when they return to a community setting.

In Massachusetts, the Homeward Bound program would have liked to develop a community follow-up component, but they have been prevented from doing so because they would be usurping the role of the regular DYS caseworkers. This kind of concession to the bureaucratic turf lines is one of the reasons that innovative programs are harder to develop in public agencies.

Of course effective continuity of care requires more than simple organizational arrangements. The residential program staff must be motivated to incorporate family and community issues into the treatment program and community caseworkers must stay in touch with what goes on in the programs and pick up where the residential program leaves off. This kind of case continuity is facilitated in many private programs by their small size, unique program culture, and strong professional and social ties among the program staff.

OTHER TYPES OF PROGRAMS

In Massachusetts and Pennsylvania, two states that have been heavy users of private sector programs, there has been a move away from traditional large scale training schools, even for those youths for whom the system requires secure confinement.[9] Their new secure facilities now consist of several small 12 to 15 bed facilities, with at least a one-to-one staff ratio. The small size and heavy staffing ratio keep these facilities from developing the kind of negative peer culture that pervades larger institutions. Further, the staff can maintain much stricter controls over youths who are prone to act out.

In addition to wilderness and small secure programs, several types of community programs are currently being used as alternatives to incarceration. The most innovative of these are forms of intensive supervision in which community people are hired to work with and supervise three or four youths who continue to reside in their community. In Massachusetts the Key Program runs such a program in 200 communities using college graduates who develop behavioral contracts with each youth, maintaining strict supervision and helping to resolve family, school, or employment problems. In Dade County, Florida, community people have been hired to work with adjudicated youths on a one-to-

---

[9]There is still a great deal of controversy over how many secure beds are really needed, given the existence of the many alternative residential options. A study by Krisberg and Schwartz (1983) showed that individual states varied in their admissions to state training schools, as a percentage of the population at risk, by many orders of magnitude. California, Arizona, and Washington admit more than 400 per 100,000 population, but Colorado, Michigan, and Illinois admit fewer than 150; and Pennsylvania, New Jersey, and Massachusetts admit fewer than 100.

one basis. The emphasis of that program is on street contacts and not office paperwork.

POST-PROGRAM CONTACTS: LEAVING
THE NEST PROBLEMS

As long as a substantial number of youths continue to recidivate following their release from any type of intensive or residential program, there will be the issue of whether they should have remained under program supervision for a longer period. This is especially true if there have been dramatic improvements in a youth's behavior and attitude while he or she was in the program.

A natural tendency among program operators is to believe that more is better; if they cannot succeed with a particular youth in six months, then maybe in a year they can do better. This belief can lead to a gradual stretching out of average program duration far in excess of that originally planned. This happened with the California Youth Authority's Community Treatment Project (Lerman, 1975) and the English Borstal system (Hawkins and Zimring, 1985).

However, modest changes in length do not appear to have any substantial effects on program outcome. The problem lies rather in the inevitable trauma of leaving the nest. In Section II we described the background characteristics and processes that lead youngsters to end up in intensive treatment programs. They frequently come from chaotic home situations. They have developed poor work habits and negative reputations in school, and have accumulated other negative habits such as the use of drugs, alcohol, gang involvement, or hanging out with delinquent peers. All of these old patterns and influences are waiting to ensnare them once again when they return home. After only a year or 18 months, not much will have changed in their home or community environment. All that a residential program can do is prepare the juvenile to deal with these problems when they come up.

Given this situation, and the fact that residential programs usually cost upward of $25,000 per year, it might be wise to maintain some supportive contacts during the post-release period for longer than the current minimal contacts. We know of no private programs that are paid to maintain supportive contacts with their charges for several years after release. Usually such contacts are assigned to regular public probation or parole officers and consist of little more than routine checks on progress.

An eighteen- or nineteen-year-old former delinquent who has just been released from strict program supervision is in a tenuous position.

There will inevitably be a lot of floundering in finding appropriate jobs or school situations and determining where and with whom they will live and what they will do with their spare time. During the first year after their release from strict program supervision they will invariably be experimenting with the wide variety of choices that are newly opened up to them. They will also find themselves in new kinds of jams, or up against frustrating situations.

Many of these youngsters would benefit from some type of counseling program—a friendly, supportive listener who was there when needed. To draw on the experience and lessons of the former residential program, the counseling program could be offered by the program operator and involve staff members who had contact with the juvenile in the program. In this way all of the work that has gone into learning about the juvenile, his or her capabilities, home situation, etc., can be brought to bear on current problems. This counseling effort might also involve occasional group sessions that would use peer support as a way of reinforcing positive behavior much on the order of Alcoholics Anonymous or some of the recently developed teenage drug rehabilitation groups.

One way to encourage (and pay for) program operators to develop this type of follow-up support would be to pay them an annual bonus for every graduate who has not been reconvicted. For instance, a payment of $1000 per youth would easily pay for a full-time counselor for 50 kids. The nonrecidivism bonus might continue for several years but decline in amount, say $500 the second year and $300 the third—reflecting the tapering off of need for any service. This kind of a bonus plan would encourage program operators to experiment with various kinds of low-level counseling, employment assistance, or tracking efforts that might prove effective in keeping more graduates from slipping back into crime.

One of the techniques a program might use to track the progress of graduates during this post-program phase would be to monitor the nature of their developing bonds. Control theory suggests that one of the major influences that keeps individuals from committing crimes is their bonds to conventional society—family, peers, and community organizations. This theory implies that one of the tasks of rehabilitation is to help a former delinquent establish such bonds. Monitoring the progress of a youth after program release should involve some attempt to monitor the nature of his bonds with particular individuals—parents, teachers, employers, counselors, and friends. A monitoring program could keep track of the identity and location of such people and periodically poll them to determine how things are going. If control theory is correct, a return to crime will often be preceded by a disruption in the offender's bonds.

In Section VI we describe a program that would benefit many young people in the 17 to 21 age range, whether a former offender or not—voluntary youth service. Such a program should be designed to serve, rather than explicitly exclude, young people with a delinquency background. Youth service programs take young people for one or two years of hard physical service, provide them with a structured work situation and living quarters away from home, and pay them a minimum wage. They are another approach to helping young people get out on their own that appears particularly appropriate for those who come from problem family backgrounds.

OTHER PROGRAM MANAGEMENT ISSUES

The most glaring deficit among all these interesting programs is the absence of any serious program evaluation effort. People continue to judge programs by what they do with juveniles in their custody, not by what the juveniles do after they leave. Knowledge about program success rates is largely anecdotal, confined to a few unrepresentative success stories of youngsters who remain in contact with the program and the few failures that come to the program's direct attention. When success rates are reported there is seldom any careful control on time at risk. The Florida Department of Human Resources counts subsequent juvenile arrests but not adult arrests. Other program evaluations present aggregate recidivism rates for everybody who has graduated from the program, lumping six-month graduates with those who have been out for two years or more. Arrests reported are frequently those "known to the program" rather than the result of any systematic record check.

To evaluate the effectiveness of any particular program, over time or compared with competing programs, it is essential to have comparable treatment groups and follow-up recidivism data.[10] Otherwise any apparent differences in success rates, which could be important for policy decisions, may only reflect the effects of selection bias or different follow-up reporting procedures. The most accurate method of ensuring comparable treatment groups across competitive programs involves

---

[10]Recidivism data at a minimum should include the date, charge, and disposition of all subsequent arrests. Analyses of these data should distinguish among offenders according to the seriousness of their charges, time to first arrest or conviction, and the frequency of arrests over a sustained period.

random assignment, so that each juvenile has an equal chance of being assigned to either program.

Other important issues that must be confronted as the number of available programs proliferate include whether program participation should be voluntary or mandatory and the basis for regulation. The VisionQuest and Homeward Bound programs take only volunteers. AMI takes juveniles who "volunteer" only to escape much more severe punishment by the adult system. VisionQuest does not let participants back out once they begin the program. AMI will remove a youth who is not cooperating with the program. Research is needed to determine if either of these approaches is preferable or if one is more appropriate for a particular type of youth.

VI. PROMISING PROGRAMS FOR ALL KIDS

Section V described several interesting programs for fairly serious delinquents, those who were past the point where "home on probation" was not enough. This section deals with a much broader category of "kids at risk," those who exhibit the preliminary behavior or background characteristics that are predictive of future delinquency but who are not currently before the court as adjudicated delinquents, and those who have completed their participation in court-mandated treatment programs and have returned to their homes.

It is generally accepted, although not proven, that the earlier a youngster's antisocial behavior patterns are addressed, the easier they will be to modify. Early intervention efforts also hold the promise of reducing the problems caused later for both the child and the community.

The arguments arise over who should do the intervening and under what rationale. Intervention, meaning efforts to control behavior, by parents is generally applauded, but efforts by "authorities" are not, unless the behavior of the child has reached certain threshold levels. Even here, interventions by authorities are limited to narrowly prescribed efforts designed to curb specific behaviors that are disruptive in specific situations. Authorities (school, police, court, welfare) have nowhere near the broad repertoire of interventions at their disposal that are held by some parents, nor are they able to set the same kind of behavioral standards. Until the child's behavior has escalated up to clear criminal conduct, public authorities are increasingly circumscribed to pursue only those disciplinary objectives that are reasonably related to the achievement of other program goals, such as education or the child's safety, narrowly defined.

Therefore, programs that prevent delinquency must do so in the name of other goals such as general child service or improved academic achievement. Furthermore, the delinquency prevention objectives of these programs cannot be made transparent by narrow targeting. Programs must be designed to help all kids who suffer from a particular disadvantage, not just those who are predicted to be at risk for crime (M. Miller, 1985b).

Four program categories that lie outside the formal juvenile justice system network appear to be helpful in curbing the delinquent or antisocial behavior of kids at risk. They are:

1. Preschool programs such as Headstart;
2. Parent training programs such as that developed at the Oregon Social Learning Center;
3. School programs designed to enhance the achievement of low income children, and
4. Voluntary youth service programs such as the California Conservation Corps, which allows young people to serve society while obtaining work experience.

These are programs from which many children could benefit, not just those who are at risk for delinquency. Their primary effects on the youngsters that are exposed to them are improved performance in school or job readiness. There is no obvious method or rationale for singling out particular kids, based on their delinquent behavior and perceived risk, for participation in these programs without a large number of false positives. Given the potential benefits, there is no justification for excluding juveniles who do not exhibit behavioral problems but who suffer from the same social, economic or physical disadvantages.

In addition to the programs listed above, a comprehensive list of programs that might reduce the likelihood of later delinquency for high-risk populations or reduce the number of high-risk children being born would include:

1. More extensive sex education, counseling, and access to birth control for high-risk teenage girls, based on the notion that many delinquents are children born to parents who were not yet prepared to raise them properly;
2. Parent education classes for high-risk teenagers and parents-to-be, assuming that these classes can create more effective parents;
3. More extensive prenatal and postnatal medical care for high-risk mothers and offspring, based on the assumption that this care will reduce the number of children with physiological deficits that impede social learning;
4. More extensive investigative resources and family therapy programs to respond to reported instances of child abuse, on the assumption that abusive behavior by parents promotes delinquency and is responsive to treatment.

We chose to write up these four program types because their potential effects on crime are becoming well understood. However, they extend well beyond the scope of OJJDP's traditional programmatic concerns. This is not to suggest that OJJDP should become a primary actor in the provision of early childhood education or implementation of educational reforms. These are areas in which other federal agencies must take the lead. However, recognition of these legitimate policy boundaries need not prevent OJJDP from adopting an activist stance in encouraging program initiation in these areas nor from ensuring that the needs of high-risk youth are being served.

PRESCHOOL PROGRAMS

Children from low-income families are likely to have problems adjusting to the demands of school settings in several ways. Their parents are unlikely to have provided them with educational toys, games, and books or to have worked with them on reading and language skills. They may also have been unused to the kind of discipline required in a classroom setting and less able to interact with other children in a cooperative manner. They may also have received less warmth and affection from adults and therefore be more insecure and less willing to try new things. Finally, poor children are more likely to suffer from physiological handicaps or inadequate diets.

Any of these problems can cause a child to progress much slower than his peers in the classroom and to have problems getting along with other children. Poor classroom achievement and rejection by conventional peers are both factors that are thought to place a child at risk for later delinquency and dropping out of school.

The most logical type of program for dealing with the problems of poor classroom preparedness and inadequate socialization are programs that work with these children before they enter school. Such programs engender little parent resistance and are not disruptive of traditional parental roles. They reach children between 3 and 5 years of age at a time when they are ready to begin developing basic skills and are capable of interacting with their peers, and when the alternative for many would be long hours of watching TV with little supervision. In a nutshell, early education and daycare programs offer opportunities for stimulation and socialization with conventional peers that can overcome the effects of familial deficiencies in this area.

But do they work? Evaluations of Headstart programs suggest that they do. Results from six longitudinal evaluations provide strong evidence that early education significantly reduced the number of low-income children that were later assigned to special education classes. (U.S. Department of Health, Education and Welfare, 1978). In several of the evaluations the percentage of children who were later assigned to special education classes was reduced by at least half: 54 to 23 percent;

29 to 3 percent; 28 to 14 percent. Preschool students were also less likely to be held back a grade or to be rated underachieving on the basis of minimal performance tests. Preschool children were also more likely than others to give achievement related reasons for being proud of themselves.

An evaluation of one preschool program that dealt with minority children in Ypsilanti, Michigan (Berrueta-Clement et al., 1984) shows that such programs can greatly affect subsequent delinquent behavior. The Perry Preschool Program was begun in the early 1960s as a local attempt to solve a local problem of school failure and delinquency on the part of the disadvantaged segment of the school population. The study covers 123 black youths who were randomly assigned to either a high quality two-year preschool program (the Perry Preschool) or no preschool at all, during five successive years. Those who attended preschool had better grades, fewer failing marks, and fewer absences in elementary school. They required fewer special education services and were more likely to graduate from high school. They were more likely to continue their education after high school and more likely to be employed by age 19. More to the point, children who had attended preschool were rated by their teachers as having better classroom conduct than their counterparts. By age 19 those who had attended preschool were less likely to have been arrested (31 versus 51 percent), less likely to have experienced more than two arrests (12 versus 25 percent), and self-reported fewer total offenses. The authors of the Ypsilanti study estimate that a taxpayer investment in a preschool program would return benefits over a 15-year period with a present worth exceeding $28,000.

PARENT TRAINING

Many of the youths who go on to become chronic offenders are first identified as troublesome youngsters by their teachers, parents, and even their peers, when they are between the ages of 6 and 12. Their troublesome behavior may include excessive aggressiveness, inattention at school, stealing, lying, or resistance to adult authority. Some of this behavior may be due to ineffective childrearing practices by the child's parents, or to some biological abnormality that interferes with social learning ability or ability to control emotions or behavior. If their troublesomeness continues, many of these youths will drop further behind their peers in academic achievements and social skills. Their school attendance may begin to drop off as they drift into deviant peer groups.

At this time the program for dealing with such youngsters that is receiving the most attention is the parent training program of the Oregon Social Learning Center (Wilson, 1983), which has evolved out of more than a decade of continuing research. It trains parents in techniques for monitoring and changing their children's bad behavior (Wiltz and Patterson, 1974). Evaluations have shown that the OSLC parent-training techniques reduce targeted behaviors more effectively than do conventional therapies (Patterson, Cobb, and Ray, 1973; Walter and Gilmore, 1973; Wiltz and Patterson, 1974); the effects of the training are generalized to other siblings (Arnold, Levine, and Patterson, 1975), to nontargeted deviant behaviors (Patterson 1974a, 1974b, 1975), and to reductions in disruptive classroom behaviors; and that effects persist over 4 to 13 month intervals for two criterion measures of deviant behavior—observed rates and parent reports (Patterson and Fleischman, 1979).

The training program, which utilizes behavior modification techniques, is based on research by the OSLC staff showing how disruptive children interact with their families. For instance, Patterson (1976) describes a sequence in which a child's disruptive behavior accelerates (yelling, hitting, refusing to follow instructions, etc.) when opposed by the parents. The child in fact has learned how to manipulate his environment by using bursts of disruptive behavior to overwhelm the adults who would discipline him.

According to Wiltz and Patterson, 1974, parents are asked to read the programmed text *Living with Children*, by Patterson and Gullion (1968). The parents are then asked to select several child behaviors to be changed. Parents are given specific instructions for observing and counting the frequency of disruptive behavior. After they have demonstrated a willingness and ability to collect and report baseline data by phone, they are invited to join a small group of other parents also participating in the training. Weekly group meetings involve no more than five sets of parents and up to four therapists, all of whom have Master's level training and at least one year of experience.

Comparisons of outcome results with similar parent-training programs suggest that using trained therapists rather than graduate students is essential in meeting client resistance and dealing with related family problems, such as marital discord and depression. Another apparently critical component of the OSLC program is that it is not time-limited: parents get as much training as they need. In one evaluation (Patterson, Chamberlain, and Reid, 1982) the average therapist time per family was 17 hours, but ranged from 4 to 48 hours across ten families in the group. The week-by-week progress for each child is charted.

When the targeted behavior has come under control, the parents select a second target behavior and devise their own program. The therapist observes and assists. Criterion measures that are used to assess baseline and post-program behavior are the *Family Interaction Coding System (FICS)*, a 29-category observation system designed to sequentially sample ongoing family interactions, the *Total Aversive Behavior (TAB)* score, the sum of 14 noxious behavior categories, expressed as a rate (of adverse behavior) per minute, and the *Parent Daily Report (PDR)*, a 34-item problem behavior checklist designed to assess the frequency of symptoms during a 24-hour period. During the training, the PDR is taken over the phone five times a week.

The techniques in which the parents are trained include monitoring and recording the child's behavior; administering contingent punishments, such as "time outs" (being made to sit quietly for two minutes) or loss of privileges; and rewarding positive behavior in a consistent way.

The OSLC parent-training therapy has been shown to result in an average 63 percent reduction in mean rate of deviant behavior (from a baseline mean TAB score of .92 deviant acts per minute) compared with a 17 percent reduction resulting from conventional therapies (Patterson, Chamberlain, and Reid, 1982). Patterson (1976, p. 306) believes that about one-third of the families who are referred to the clinic just need the specific behavior modification skills, another third need to be taught negotiation skills to resolve marital conflicts and personal problems, and one-third will fail no matter what is done.

The OSLC treatment has not been shown to be as effective for "stealers" as for "social aggressors." A four-year followup of one treatment group showed that treated "stealers" were no less likely to be arrested than nontreated stealers (Moore, Chamberlain, and Mukai, 1979). Other analyses show that families of "stealers" are more likely to drop out of the program than families of social aggressors.

Some major problems still need to be resolved before the OSLC parent training techniques can be said to provide the basis for a systematic intervention strategy. First, the techniques must be tested with a more criminogenic population than they have been to date. Eugene, Oregon, where OSLC is located, and from which most of its test families have been drawn, is a far cry from the poor inner-city neighborhoods of New York, Chicago, or Los Angeles. Second, the effectiveness of the treatment depends heavily on the skill of the therapists in devising strategies for overcoming parental resistance to the techniques required, so it remains to be shown whether these skills can effectively be disseminated to others. It just might be that the unique setting (Eugene, Oregon has been rated among the nation's most desirable cities to live in) and supportive working conditions at OSLC are able to attract a caliber of staff that would not as easily be drawn to a large-scale urban program.

OSLC's work to date has been supported primarily by federal research grants. Any large-scale application of the techniques would require some attention to the problem of targeting and recruiting the most recalcitrant parents and determining how the training would be paid for. To make the program available to a wider poverty clientele, it will probably be necessary to substitute paraprofessionals and volunteers for the highly trained therapists currently used by OSLC.

The OSLC technique offers a strategy for assisting parents who will recognize their child's behavioral problems and are willing to try to change them. They offer no assistance when parents refuse to acknowledge adverse behavior or when they are incapable or unwilling to apply the techniques that parent training requires.

EFFECTIVE SCHOOLS

If parents are unable or unwilling to deal with the pre-delinquent adverse behavior of their children, the only other acceptable institutions for doing so are the schools. Only they have sufficient contact, resources, and authority to mount any serious systematic delinquency prevention efforts that will reach the children who are most at risk. However, the development of effective programs that meet both the needs of children at risk and the "due process" and "equality of treatment" standard articulated in recent school cases may be far from a simple matter (see M. Miller, 1985b).

One of the main complaints raised by critics of urban public school systems is that they fail to meet the special needs of the inner-city minority poor. In many inner-city schools more than 20 percent of students are absent on any given day; a substantial fraction drop out before graduation, and many who do graduate are deficient in the basic skills required for employment or further education.

It has been a matter of philosophical debate as to whether these problems, which are clearly demonstrated by attendance and achievement data, can be solved by schools. Some analysts (Coleman et al., 1966; Jencks, 1972) have argued that academic achievement is determined largely by the child's personal characteristics and family background and only marginally by the type and quality of educational programs to which they are exposed. Others (Edmonds and Frederikson, 1978) argue that the failure to find consistent evidence of positive affects of school programs on academic achievement is due to inadequacies in the program rather than inability of poor children to benefit.

In recent years the search for effective compensatory educational techniques has shifted somewhat away from the top-down research and development approach (theory yields program designs, which lead to demonstrations and evaluations, which yield new findings, which lead to revisions in theory, etc.) to the study of what have been called "instructionally effective schools"—schools in which poor children do show much larger gains in achievement scores than would be predicted by their personal and family characteristics (Kimbrough, 1985).

Instructionally effective schools have been found to be characterized by high staff commitment to student achievement and sense of efficacy, the communication of high expectations to students; orderly and purposeful classrooms, high levels of parent/teacher and parent/principal contact, on-going inservice training and frequent informal consultation, strong leadership by principals and teacher autonomy, flexibility by teachers in adopting instructional techniques, more time devoted to direct instruction, use of competitive academic teams, and consistent appropriate reinforcement (Armor et al., 1976; Brookover et al., 1979; Weber, 1971; Rutter et al., 1979).

In studies that focused specifically on discipline problems, schools with good discipline and low rates of misbehavior were characterized by participatory decisionmaking and governance, strong and effective leadership by the principal, clear rules of conduct combined with firm and consistent discipline, student and staff identification with bonding to the school, the use of symbols of identity and excellence and rewards for achievement, and cohesion and coordination between administration and staff (Wayson and Lasley, 1984; NIE, 1978).

The traditional approach to problem behavior in the public schools has been based on an individual psychopathology or medical model. The disruptive child is assumed to have some special temperament or character traits that cause his or her behavior problems. The solution was counseling and escalating penalties. First such children are ordered to leave the classroom and wait in the hall, next they are sent to the principal, the parents are called in for a conference, then suspension and finally expulsion. The really troublesome kids end up excluded from school or attending special schools for troublemakers.

The new approach to handling disruptive behavior assumes that there is some interaction among the classroom setting, the program, and children's behavior. More emphasis is placed on establishing environments in which negative behavior is naturally discouraged and the child's interests are engaged. In schools where these techniques have been applied, attendance rates and achievement scores have improved considerably and evidence of disruptive behavior—such as vandalism, graffiti, and assaults—decline precipitously (Kimbrough, 1985).

The establishment of the required school climate and programs is no simple matter. Experience has shown that a dedicated and gifted principal is necessary to pull it off. The motivation for establishing such a school must come from within the school community. It cannot be ordered from the outside. Clearly, one of the roles that instructionally effective schools can serve is to provide a standard against which other schools can be measured. Everybody agrees we need better schools for poor children. The effective schools research may demonstrate that they are not beyond our grasp.

YOUTH SERVICE PROGRAMS

It is impossible to talk with young people in the 18-to-20 age range without sensing a high degree of ambivalence. Unless they are embarked in very clear academic or vocational career patterns, which most ex-juvenile offenders are not, their lives are pretty much up in the air. They are not yet ready to commit to any one particular career area; and besides, interesting jobs that hold some promise of a future are hard to find. They tend to bounce around in marginal occupations and part-time work. They are not sure whether they want to live at home or out on their own; and their parents are not sure that they want them. If they have been off in some residential program they are also involved in reestablishing a social life, particularly as it involves the opposite sex.

Graduates of residential treatment programs are really just big kids who still have lots of experimenting and growing up to do. They face many rude shocks as they try to find their economic and social roles in the community. Unfortunately, many of them do not make it without turning back to crime. This is particularly frustrating when the individual appears to have made such positive strides and engendered such high hopes while they were enrolled in a residential program. But these youths come from and go back to poor family situations and delinquent peer groups when they are released. It is not so surprising that old influences re-ignite old patterns of behavior.

One solution that comes to mind for dealing with the "youth at loose ends" problem is to provide some kind of continued programming for these youths after they return to the community. The problem is how to do this in a way that is fair to all youths with similar problems, and does not simply increase the amount of time the youth is under juvenile or criminal justice control. One candidate for this role is some form of voluntary or universal youth service program that would accept these youths for one or two years of public service in return for minimum wages, possibly room and board, and possibly some educational or other entitlement upon successful completion of the program. The primary benefit that youths would be expected to derive from involvement in such programs would be general work experience and the experience of living and working with other young adults away from home. The California Conservation Corps is one such program. Others exist or are being planned in San Francisco and New York City. As the country begins to contemplate the shrinkage of the available labor pool of those in this age range, it is likely that various voluntary service plans will be receiving even greater attention.

VII. THE ECONOMICS OF EARLY INTERVENTION

It is common practice for after-dinner speakers, in addressing an audience of criminal justice practitioners or researchers, to declare their support for early intervention efforts. The real answer to prison overcrowding or high recidivism rates, or high-rate offenders, they claim, is to change behavior before the individual has become "entrenched in a life of crime." Unfortunately this strategy is easier to propose than execute. The amount of effort devoted to programs that would seem to qualify as early intervention efforts, whether prevention or rehabilitation, has been in a state of decline for the past decade, partly because of the absence of clear proof that such efforts do any good at all in reducing subsequent delinquency and partly because of a growing disinclination of government at all levels to spend money on social programs directed primarily at the poor (Children's Defense Fund, 1984).

Early intervention efforts can be justified on at least two grounds:

1. Benefits to the offenders treated in terms of improved quality of life.
2. Benefits to society at large in terms of reduced crime and costs of incarceration.

Benefits to offenders are somewhat subjective in that they involve reduced risks of incarceration, depression, alcoholism, and other adverse consequences (Robins, 1966). Furthermore, not everyone would agree that public funds should be spent simply to improve the prospects of potential offenders. However, the benefits to society of reduced crime and incarceration costs are clear and direct and therefore can be used as a benchmark for estimating how successful early intervention programs must be to justify their expense.

Peter Rydell (1985) has performed such an analysis, comparing the effectiveness of rehabilitation programs for chronic juvenile offenders with selective incapacitation as alternative means of reducing crime. The analysis proceeds as follows.

Step 1: He estimates arrest rates, incarceration rates, average time served, and cost of confinement for juvenile and adult offenders (national averages) under current policies.

Step 2: He estimates the increase in offenders incarcerated and decrease in crime that would result from a selective incapacitation policy of doubling the sentences for adults who are predicted to be high-rate offenders.

Step 3: He determines how effective a rehabilitation program for chronic juvenile offenders must be in order to reduce crime rates as much as the selective incapacitation policy evaluated in Step 2.

Step 4: He estimates the cost saving in reduced incarceration that would result from the rehabilitation program in Step 3 and therefore be available to spend on rehabilitation.

Incapacitation is selected as the standard for comparing with intervention efforts because it is the only offender-focused strategy of crime reduction for which there is supporting evidence at this time (Blumstein, Cohen, and Nagin, 1978). Selective incapacitation is the most efficient use of incapacitation and provides a conservative standard against which treatment programs can be compared (Greenwood and Abrahamse, 1982).

This analysis does not evaluate any particular rehabilitation program. Rather it establishes a lower bound on program effectiveness and an upper bound on program costs, both of which must be met if a rehabilitation program is to be more effective than selective incapacitation in reducing crime rates on a straight cost comparison basis.

The analysis begins by assuming that there are two types of offenders: high-rate offenders who account for 15 percent of the offender population and commit on the average 273 index crimes per year; low-rate offenders who represent 85 percent of the offender population and commit 24 crimes per year.[1] Probabilities of arrest and incarceration and confinement times and costs for index crimes, based on national averages, are presented in Table 3.[2]

Using the Shinnar and Shinnar (1975) model as modified by Greenwood and Abrahamse (1982) to estimate the effects of selective incapacitation policies, Table 4 shows the estimated fraction of active offenders who are incarcerated at any one time, and the total number of offenders. The amount of crime attributable to the different types of offenders is shown in Table 5. The proportion of crimes attributable to juvenile offenders is somewhat lower than that reflected in arrest statistics because juvenile offenders are more likely to commit crimes in groups.

---

[1] Based on self-reported offense rates from the Rand Inmate Survey (Chaiken and Chaiken, 1982).

[2] Derived from data in the 1982 *Sourcebook of Criminal Justice Statistics* (Flanagan and McLeod, 1983).

Table 3

PARAMETERS OF CURRENT CRIMINAL JUSTICE SYSTEM
PERFORMANCE FOR INDEX OFFENDERS

	Juveniles	Adults
Probability of arrest per crime	0.04	0.04
Probability of commitment, given arrest	0.13	0.16
Average time served (years)	0.6	1.6
Average cost per inmate year	$21,927	$19,359

Table 4

FRACTION OF OFFENDERS INCARCERATED

Type of Offender	Juvenile	Adult
High rate	.44	.74
Low rate	.07	.20
Total offenders (in thousands)	491	1,345

Table 5

TOTAL NUMBER OF CRIMES PER YEAR
COMMITTED BY DIFFERENT TYPES
OF OFFENDERS
(In thousands)

Type of Offender	Juvenile	Adult
High rate	5,620	9,720
Low rate	4,680	14,710
Total	10,300	24,430

Policies of selective incapacitation involve giving longer terms to predicted high-rate offenders (Greenwood and Abrahamse, 1982; Cohen, 1983). The policy tested by Rydell involves sentencing all adult defendants who are predicted to be high-rate offenders to terms that are double the current average: 3.2 years rather than 1.6. The analysis is performed assuming a one-third accuracy rate in predicting high-rate offenders (one-third of those predicted to be high-rate offenders actually are), which is typical of the accuracy achieved in prediction studies (Monahan et al., 1981). Table 6 shows how many offenders would be incarcerated under the selective policy compared with those under current practice, and the resulting crime rate. With selective sentencing and one-third prediction accuracy the number of incarcerated offenders would increase by 5.9 percent and the crime rate would be decreased by 4.8 percent. If the prediction accuracy were increased to one-half, which appears to be about the maximum accuracy attainable, the number of offenders incarcerated under the selective policy would increase over current practice by only 5.7 percent and the crime rate would decrease by 6.6 percent.

An effective early intervention program might work by reducing the future offense rates of all offenders proportionately, or by reducing the offense rates of some to zero and leaving those of others unchanged, or any combination in between. Rydell assumed the first situation applied, the conservative approach. If treatment programs actually ter-

Table 6

NUMBER OF INCARCERATED OFFENDERS, AND
CRIMES UNDER CURRENT AND SELECTIVE
SENTENCING POLICIES
(In thousands)

	Current Practices	Selective Sentencing
Juveniles incarcerated	60.1	60.1
Adults incarcerated		
High rate	148.5	156.1
Low rate	224.7	242.5
Total	433.3	458.7 (up 5.9%)
Total Crimes (millions)	34.73	33.08 (down 4.8%)

minate the career of some offenders and leave the offense rates of others unchanged, the incapacitation effects of any selective sentencing policy will be larger in subsequent years than if all offenders remained active at lower rates, because there will be fewer active offenders each with higher average offense rates.

By trial and error Rydell estimated that in order to reduce crime by the same 4.8 percent as the selective incapacitation policy, a rehabilitation program for those juvenile offenders who were predicted to be chronics would have to reduce future offense rates by 37 percent under what they would have been if no intervention were applied. If this reduction in offense rates were achieved, then the total number of offenders that would be incarcerated in future years would decline by 4.3 percent, a reduction of approximately 19,000 inmates. The cost saving produced by this reduction in inmate population would amount to approximately $851 million. If all of this money were used to support rehabilitation programs for predicted chronic juvenile offenders it would provide approximately $28,800 per juvenile treated, assuming that twice the actual number of true chronics must be treated in order to ensure that most of the true chronics are included in the program.

The minimum level of program effectiveness required would not be as high if the alternative means of crime reduction were a general incapacitation approach, nor would it be as high if the rehabilitation effects were selective rather than general—reducing the offense rates of some offenders much more than others. Even earlier intervention efforts would not need to be quite as effective, because they would prevent a greater amount of juvenile crime, but they would need to reach a much larger number of potential offenders (because the predictability of chronics is less accurate at a younger age) and have proportionately less to spend on each one.

This analysis is only a first step in illustrating how it is possible to compare alternative intervention strategies at different stages in criminal careers. If information concerning the relative effectiveness of different strategies were actually available it would be possible to perform a much more detailed analysis, possibly by computer simulation of actual careers, to allow for more accurate representation of the offender population and actual career progressions.

VIII. CONCLUSIONS AND POLICY IMPLICATIONS

This report has provided evidence to convince the reader that rehabilitation and prevention are not entirely dead. The seeds of chronic delinquency were shown to be planted at an early age in a breakdown of the normal socializing processes. This breakdown is usually a result of incompetent or inattentive parental behavior and may be aggravated by a child's abnormal physiological or psychological characteristics. Inadequate early socialization leads to failure in school, rejection by conventional peers, and continuing drift in deviant activities and peer groups. By the time a juvenile court clearly identifies a juvenile as a chronic or serious delinquent, he or she will have fallen far behind more conventional peers in social, academic, and emotional development. Intervention efforts will continue to be hampered by problems within the juvenile's family and the necessity of facing the normal problems of later adolescence.

Prediction studies suggest that future chronic offenders can be identified at about age 13 on the basis of their early offenses, school record, and their family's characteristics and behavior. However, coercive programming under the formal jurisdiction of the juvenile court is limited by both legal and practical concerns to those juveniles who have been found guilty of real criminal acts. Preventive programming for high-risk youths who have not yet been found to have committed criminal acts must take place within the educational system or community. Programs that show promise of reducing the risk of later delinquency for high-risk children include early education programs such as Headstart, parent training programs such as that developed by the Oregon Social Learning Center, and educational programs and practices identified in the "effective schools" and "safe schools" literature. All of these programs focus on high-risk populations, are acceptable to parents, and show evidence of effectiveness.

For adjudicated delinquents, programs that are receiving the most favorable attention currently are those that substitute isolation in remote wilderness settings and physical challenges for traditional programs emphasizing academic and vocational training in secure settings. Most of these new programs have been developed by private contractors for particular judges or corrections administrators who were looking for alternatives to traditional training schools associated with negative peer influences and high recidivism rates. Because of their increased emphasis on treatment effectiveness, some of these new programs have developed multi-phased programs (extending from secure or isolated residential settings, to group homes, family counseling and community reentry) that appear more suited to the needs of their clientele than does secure custody alone.

What we hope to leave the reader with is some feeling of optimism and support for the changes that are taking place. We have tried to show why we consider the "nothing works" conclusion to be simplistic overreaction to the empirical evidence, and how early intervention programs might compete with incapacitation as effective crime control strategies.

In this final section we concentrate on a few specific recommendations that we believe can improve the quality of the rehabilitative programming that is available. They are not all that should be done, but only the first steps. The task of developing and sustaining effective treatment programs will require constant attention.

PROGRAM EVALUATION

If we have learned anything in this review it is that the development and continuing operation of effective treatment programs for delinquent juveniles is difficult and demanding work. It requires strong leadership, dedicated and competent staff, a willingness to experiment continuously and to advocate controversial positions, and an ability to earn the respect and affections of the juvenile while maintaining a firm disciplinary atmosphere.

These conditions are not easy to create or maintain. Yet without them, a program is not likely to be much better than no program at all. In order to raise the quality of programs to which serious juvenile offenders are exposed, more effort must be devoted to the continuing assessment of program effects. This evaluation effort is required to determine which among the many programs currently available are most effective, and to ensure that they remain effective once identified. Without the pressure provided by systematic impact assessment, historical experience suggests that most programs will concentrate on minimizing custodial problems rather than promoting long-term behavioral change.

The early stages of developing systematic program evaluation techniques also require that random assignment of some youths between experimental and comparison programs be made to ensure that outcomes are not contaminated by selection bias. If judges or correctional caseworkers are allowed to exclude certain categories of youths from one program but not others, or if program assignments are made on the basis of which youths might best benefit from particular programs, then it will be extremely difficult to determine whether observed differences in subsequent recidivism rates and between participants in experimental and comparison programs are due to differences in program effectiveness or assignment practices. If one program is viewed as more beneficial than others it is inevitable that judges and caseworkers will attempt to send the more promising (or amenable) youths to what is thought to be the better program. This situation is likely to occur when a new program is being compared with those in existing training schools and will clearly favor the experimental program in any subsequent comparison.

When there has been an accumulated body of data that can predict subsequent recidivism rates for different categories of juveniles based on their personal characteristics, family background, and previous behavior, it will be possible to relax the requirement for random assignment and control for selection bias by taking these predictive factors into account.

OJJDP can take several actions to promote this evaluation effort. First, it can sponsor some evaluations on its own. This would be particularly helpful in areas where there are several competitive or controversial new programs, as is now the case with private sector programs for chronic offenders. A series of OJJDP sponsored evaluations would help clarify some of the conflicting claims that are being made about the effectiveness of these programs and would also make practitioners more aware of the need for evaluation of their programs.

Second, OJJDP can promote the wider use of evaluations among state and local programs by making practitioners aware of the need, and providing a forum in its publications or in special workshops or conferences convened for this purpose.

Third, in the future it may be appropriate for OJJDP to establish and fund a National Center for the Evaluation of Delinquency Programs, which could act as a clearinghouse, coordinator, and technical consultant for the design and collection of program outcome data, and which would analyze and publish the final results. This Center, a nonprofit agency devoted to program evaluation, should be run by a Board of Directors consisting of practitioners representing judges, probation officers, and public and private correctional program administrators. In time this Center might become self-supporting by selling its evaluation services on a pro rata basis, say by charging each program to collect and evaluate followup data for each juvenile, along with requiring certain background data on each subject. Such a center would need at least $500,000 to $750,000 in funding per year to carry out this role. In addition to determining the effectiveness of specific programs, this ongoing evaluation effort would also be able to gradually determine which approaches to treatment proved beneficial for particular types of juveniles.

At this time there is very little serious evaluation effort taking place within the juvenile offender treatment area. Most programs feel extremely strapped for resources. Because nobody else is devoting attention to program evaluation, there is little motivation to spend money when it is needed elsewhere. It is also true that small programs cannot support or provide an adequate climate for such evaluation efforts to take place. Pooling the evaluation efforts of many programs in a consortium makes sense from both a financial and program management standpoint. A single Center could perform the evaluation more cheaply, and with more integrity, than could individual programs on their own.

BIOLOGICAL STUDIES

Some more focused effort should be devoted to determining the role that biological factors can or should play in the assignment of juveniles to treatment programs, or to the evaluation of treatment outcomes. Our knowledge about the interactions between biology and criminal behavior currently consists of no more than a series of weak correlations between various measures of criminal behavior and an almost random assortment of biological variables (Freier, 1985). The data are derived largely from studies of incarcerated populations or minor offenders in Scandinavian countries, which have very different patterns of criminal behavior than here in the United States.

We know little about how these biological factors can improve our ability to predict future behavior over and above what can be done with the usual socioeconomic and behavioral variables. Even if they can make a contribution, current policies leave little room for the use of such predictive power. As we have argued in Section IV, preventive programs must be broadly targeted to remain nonpejorative. Assignment to coercive treatment programs must be based on explicit criminal behavior. However, there is room for biological variables to guide practitioners in the assignment of juveniles to specific programs (Van Duesen, 1985). More effort should be devoted to determining which variables are useful for this purpose and how they should be used.

Research concerning the relationship between biological variables and criminality in recent years has been plagued by an unusually high degree of controversy because of past abuses in the area, and possibly because of the strong sociological or psychological orientation of most academic criminologists. It would be extremely helpful in defusing this controversy if work in this area were to be undertaken by a wider set of researchers than in the past, and if that work were better integrated with more traditional types of criminological studies. Some thought should be given to establishing a special peer review panel to plan and review work in this area. In summary, research concerning biological influences on criminal behavior should be integrated into longitudinal studies examining the full range of causal factors.

LONGITUDINAL STUDIES

We need more longitudinal studies that examine cohorts of high-risk groups and provide an opportunity to access the effects of early intervention activities. For these cohort studies to be most useful (1) they must collect information on background variables that have been found to be predictive of chronic delinquency in the past; (2) some of the subjects should participate in potentially valuable early intervention programs, such as preschool programs, parent training efforts, or special school programs, in such a way that the results are not entirely contaminated by selection bias; and (3) some of the delinquent members of the cohort should be assigned to experimental treatment programs on a random assignment basis.

As in the study of biological contributions to criminality, it might be helpful if a broadly representative peer review panel planned or reviewed the work in this area. Members should be selected on the basis of their own demonstrated expertise and interest, rather than committing all of the funds required for such a large undertaking to a single research group.

EXPLORATION OF EXTENDED COMMUNITY PROGRAMMING MODELS

Even with the minimal followup data currently available, many of the new private sector programs may do a far better job of improving the behavior and attitude of the delinquents assigned to them at the time of release than they do a year or more after the youths have left the program. Treatment effects invariably wash out under the pressure of community, family, and peer group influence. Rather than accepting the traditionally high failure rates experienced in dealing with chronic offenders, it might be wise to try some experiments with various forms of extended programming for high-risk categories of youth who are beyond the threshold of court-mandated programs. This is particularly important because some type of voluntary or universal youth service program will probably appear on the national political agenda within the next decade, and most current studies devote little attention to the needs or value of working with high-risk youth.

The California Conservation Corps is one model of such a program. Many others are possible. Further research is needed to determine what kinds of format should be explored.

REFERENCES

Adams, S., *Evaluative Research in Corrections: A Practical Guide,* U.S. Department of Justice, Washington, D.C., 1975.

Allen, F. A., *The Decline of the Rehabilitative Ideal: Penal Policy and Social Purpose,* Yale University Press, New Haven, 1981.

Armor, D., et al., *Analysis of the School Preferred Reading Program in Selected Los Angeles Schools,* The Rand Corporation, R-2007-LAUSD, 1976.

Armstrong, T. L., and D. M. Altschuler, *Community-Based Program Interventions for the Serious Juvenile Offender: Targeting, Strategies, and Issues,* National Center for the Assessment of Alternatives to Juvenile Justice Processing, The University of Chicago, Chicago, Illinois, February 1982.

Arnold, J., A. Levine, and G. R. Patterson, "Changes in Sibling Behavior Following Family Intervention," *Journal of Consulting and Clinical Psychology,* Vol. 43, 1975, pp. 683–688.

Averch, H. A., S. J. Carroll, T. S. Donaldson, H. J. Kiesling, and J. Pincus, *How Effective Is Schooling? A Critical Review of Research,* Educational Technology Publications, Englewood Cliffs, N.J., 1974.

Bailey, W. C., "Correctional Outcome: An Evaluation of 100 Reports," *Journal of Criminal Law, Criminology and Police Science,* Vol. 57, 1966.

Bandura, A., *Principles of Behavior Modification,* Holt, Rinehart and Winston, New York, 1968.

Bandura. A., *Social Learning Theory,* Prentice-Hall, Englewood Cliffs, N.J., 1977.

Bartollas, C., S. J. Miller, and S. Dinitz, *Juvenile Victimization: The Institutional Paradox,* John Wiley & Sons, New York, 1976.

Berman, P., and M. W. McLaughlin, *Federal Programs Supporting Educational Change: Vol. VIII, Implementing and Sustaining Innovations,* The Rand Corporation, R-1589/8-HEW, 1978.

Berrueta-Clement, J. R., L. J. Schweinhart, W. S. Barnett, A. S. Epstein, D. P. Weikhard, *Changed Lives: The Effects of the Perry Preschool Program on Youths Through Age 19,* High/Scope Educational Research Foundation, High/Scope Press, Ypsilanti, Michigan, 1984.

Blumstein, A., J. Cohen, and D. Nagin (eds.), *Deterrence and Incapacitation: Estimating the Effects of Criminal Sanctions on Crime Rates*, National Academy of Sciences, Washington, D.C., 1978.

Brookover, W. G., et al., *School Social Systems and Student Achievement: Schools Can Make a Difference*, Praeger, New York, 1979.

Chaiken, J., and M. R. Chaiken, *Varieties of Criminal Behavior*, The Rand Corporation, R-2814-NIJ, 1982.

Children's Defense Fund, "American Children in Poverty," 122 C Street, N.W., Washington, D.C., 1984.

Cloward, R. A., and L. Ohlin, *Delinquency and Opportunity: A Theory of Delinquent Gangs*, Free Press, New York, 1960.

Cohen, A. K., *Delinquent Boys: The Culture of the Gang*, Free Press, New York, 1955.

Cohen, J., "Incapacitation as a Strategy for Crime Control: Possibilities and Pitfalls," in N. Morris and M. Tonry (eds.), *Crime and Justice: An Annual Review of Literature, Vol. 4*, The University of Chicago Press, Chicago, Illinois, 1983.

Coleman, J. S., E. Q. Campbell, C. J. Hobson, J. McPartland, A. M. Mood, F. D. Weinfeld, and R. L. York, *Equality of Educational Opportunity*, U.S. Office of Education, Washington, D.C., 1966.

Edmonds, R., and J. R. Frederiksen, *Search for Effective Schools: The Identification and Analysis of City Schools that Are Instructionally Effective for Poor Children*, Harvard University, Cambridge, 1978.

Ellickson, P. L., et al., *Implementing New Ideas in Criminal Justice*, The Rand Corporation, R-2929-NIJ, 1983.

Empey, La Mar T., "Constructing Crime: Evolution and Implications of Sociological Theory," in S. M. Martin, L. B. Sechrest, and R. Redner, (eds.), *New Directions In the Rehabilitation of Criminal Offenders*, National Academy Press, Washington, D.C., 1981.

Farrington, D. P., *Further Analyses of a Longitudinal Survey of Crime and Delinquency*, Institute of Criminology, Cambridge, England, June 1983.

Farrington, D. P., and D. J. West, *The Cambridge Study in Delinquency Development*, Institute of Criminology, Cambridge, England, 1977.

Farrington, D. P., "Longitudinal Research on Crime and Delinquency," in N. Morris and M. Tonry (eds.), *Crime and Justice: An Annual Review of Research, Vol. 1*, University of Chicago Press, Chicago, Illinois, 1979.

Feld, B. C., "Criminalizing Juvenile Justice: Rules of Procedure For The Juvenile Court," *Minnesota Law Review*, Vol. 69, No. 2, December 1984.

Feld, B. C., *Neutralizing Inmate Violence,* Ballinger Publishing Company, Cambridge, Massachusetts, 1977.

Flanagan, Timothy J., and Maureen McLeod (eds.), *Sourcebook of Criminal Justice Statistics—1982,* Bureau of Justice Statistics, U.S. Department of Justice, Washington, D.C., 1983.

Freier, M., "The Biological Bases of Criminal Behavior," in P. W. Greenwood (ed.), *The Juvenile Rehabilitation Reader: The Rand Corporation,* N-2236-OJJDP (forthcoming) 1985.

Freud, S., *An Outline of Psychoanalysis,* Norton, New York, 1963.

Goddard, H. H., *Feeblemindedness: Its Causes and Consequences,* Macmillan, New York, 1914.

Goodlad, John I., *A Place Called School: Prospects for the Future,* McGraw-Hill, New York, 1984.

Goring, C., *The English Convict,* His Majesty's Stationery Office, London, England, 1913.

Greenwood, P. W. (ed.) *The Juvenile Rehabilitation Reader,* The Rand Corporation, N-2236-OJJDP (forthcoming), 1985.

Greenwood, P. W., with Allan Abrahamse, *Selective Incapacitation,* The Rand Corporation, R-2815-NIJ, 1982.

Greenwood, P. W., A. Lipson, A. Abrahamse, and F. Zimring, *Youth Crime and Juvenile Justice in California: A Report to the Legislature,* The Rand Corporation, R-3016-CSA, 1983.

Hamparian, D. M., L. Estep, S. Muntean, R. Pristino, R. Swisher, P. Wallace, J. White, *Major Issues in Juvenile Justice Information and Training: Youth in Adult Courts, Between Two Worlds,* Office of Juvenile Justice and Delinquency, U. S. Department of Justice, Washington, D.C., 1982.

Hamparian, D. M., R. Schuster, S. Dinitz, J. P. Conrad, *The Violent Few: A Study of Dangerous Juvenile Offenders,* Lexington Books, D.C. Heath and Company, Lexington, Massachusetts, 1978.

Harmeling, J. D., and M. B. Jones, "Birth Weights of High School Dropouts," *Am. J. Orthopsychiatry,* Vol. 38, 1968, pp. 63–66.

Hawkins, G. and F. Zimring, "The Treatment of Serious Youthful Offenders in Europe," in P. Greenwood (ed.), *The Juvenile Rehabilitation Reader,* The Rand Corporation, N-2236-OJJDP (forthcoming), 1985.

Hirschi, T., *Causes of Delinquency,* University of California Press, Berkeley, 1969.

Institute of Judicial Administration and the American Bar Association, *Juvenile Justice Standards Project,* Ballinger Publishing Co., Cambridge, Massachusetts, 1977 (24 vols.).

Jencks, C., *Inequality: A Reassessment of the Effect of Family and Schooling in America,* Basic Books, New York, 1972.

Kimbrough, Jackie, "School-Based Strategies for Delinquent Prevention, in P. W. Greenwood (ed.), *The Juvenile Rehabilitation Reader,* The Rand Corporation, N-2236-OJJDP (forthcoming), 1985.

Krisberg, B., and I. Schwartz, "Rethinking Juvenile Justice," *Crime and Delinquency,* July 1983.

Lerman, Paul, *Community Treatment and Social Control,* University of Chicago Press, Chicago, Illinois, 1975.

Lipton, D., R. Martinson, and J. Wilks, *The Effectiveness of Correctional Treatment: A Survey of Treatment Evaluation Studies,* Praeger, New York, 1975.

Loeber, R., and T. Dishion, "Early Predictors of Male Delinquency: A Review," *Psychological Bulletin,* Vol. 94, No. 1, 1983, pp. 68–99.

Loeber, R., T. J. Dishion, and G. R. Patterson, "Multiple Gating: A Multistage Assessment Procedure for Identifying Youths at Risk for Delinquency," *Journal of Research in Crime and Delinquency,* Vol. 21, No. 1, February 1984.

Lombroso, C., *Crime: Its Causes and Remedies,* Little Brown, Boston, 1918.

Martin, S. E., L. B. Sechrest, and R. Redner (eds.), *New Directions in the Rehabilitation of Criminal Offenders: Final Report,* National Research Council, National Academy of Sciences, Washington, D.C., 1981.

Martinson, R., "What Works? Questions and Answers About Prison Reform," *Public Interest,* Vol. 35, 1974.

McCord, J., "Some Child-rearing Antecedents of Criminal Behavior in Adult Men," *Journal of Personality and Social Psychology,* Vol. 37, 1979, pp. 1477–1486.

McKenzie, E., *Treating the Kids Nobody Wants: A Survey of Innovative Treatment Programs for Seriously Delinquent Youth,* Delta Institute, Los Angeles, August 1981.

Mednick, S. A., W. F. Gabrielli, Jr., and B. Hutchins, "Genetic Influences in Criminal Convictions: Some Evidence from an Adoption Cohort," *Science,* Vol. 224, No. 4651, 1984, pp. 891–894.

Mednick, S., and J. Volavka, "Biology and Crime," in N. Morris and M. Tonry (eds.), *Crime and Justice: An Annual Review of Research,* Vol. II, 1980.

Miller, M., "Changing Legal Paradigms in Juvenile Justice," P. W. Greenwood (ed.), *The Juvenile Rehabilitation Reader,* The Rand Corporation, N-2236-OJJDP (forthcoming) 1985a.

Miller, M., "Legal Constraints on Intervention Programs in Public Schools," in Peter W. Greenwood (ed.) *The Juvenile Rehabilitation Reader,* The Rand Corporation, N-2236-OJJDP, 1985b.

Monahan, J., S. L. Brodsky, and S. A. Shah, *Predicting Violent Behavior: An Assessment of Clinical Techniques,* Sage Publications, Beverly Hills, California, 1981.

Moore, D., P. Chamberlain, and I. Mukai, "Children at Risk for Delinquency," *Journal of Abnormal Child Psychology,* Vol. 7, No. 3, 1979.

NIE, *Violent Schools—Safe Schools,* Washington, D.C., 1978.

Osborn, S. G., and D. J. West, "The Effectiveness of Various Predictors of Criminal Careers," *Journal of Adolescence,* Vol. 1, 1978.

Patterson, G. R., "The Aggressive Child: Victim and Architect of a Coercive System," in L. A. Hamerlynck, L. C. Handy, and E. J. Mash (eds.), *Behavior Modification and Families: Theory and Research,* Vol. 1, Brunner/Mazell, New York, 1976.

Patterson, G. R., "Interventions for Boys with Conduct Problems: Multiple Setting, Treatments, and Criteria," *Journal of Consulting and Clinical Psychology,* Vol. 42, 1974a, pp. 471–481.

Patterson, G. R., "Multiple Evaluations of a Parent Training Program," in T. Thomson and W. S. Dockens, III (eds)., *Applications of Behavior Modification,* Academic Press, New York, 1975.

Patterson, G. R., "Retraining of Aggressive Boys by Their Parents: Review of Recent Literature and Follow-up Evaluations," in F. Lowry (ed.), Symposium on the Seriously Disturbed Preschool Child, *Canadian Psychiatric Association Journal,* Vol, 19, 1974b, pp. 142–161.

Patterson, G. R., *A Social Learning Approach,* Vol. 3, Castalia Publishing Company, Eugene, Oregon, 1982.

Patterson, G. R., J. A. Cobb, and R. S. Ray, *Issues and Trends in Behavior Therapy,* C. C. Thomas Publisher, Springfield, Illinois, 1973.

Patterson, G. R., P. Chamberlain, and J. B. Reid, "A Comparative Evaluation of a Parent-Training Program," *Behavior Therapy,* Vol. 13, 1982, pp. 638–650.

Patterson, G. R., and M. J. Fleischman, "Maintenance of Treatment Effects," *Behavior Therapy,* Vol. 10, 1979.

Patterson, G. R., and M. E. Gullion, *Living with Children: New Methods for Parents and Teachers,* Research Press, Champaign, Illinois, 1968.

Quinney, R., *Criminal Justice in America,* Little, Brown, Boston, 1974.

Ralph, J. H., and J. Fennessey, "Science or Reform: Some Questions About the Effective Schools Model," *Phi Delta Kappan,* June 1983.

Robins, L. N., and E. Wish, "Childhood Deviance as a Developmental Process, *Social Forces,* Vol. 56, 1977, pp. 448–473.

Robins, L. N., *Deviant Children Grow Up: A Sociological and Psychiatric Study of a Sociopathic Personality,* Williams and Williams, Baltimore, 1966.

Rosenheim, M. K., (ed.), *Pursuing Justice for the Child,* University of Chicago Press, Chicago, Illinois, 1976.

Rutter, M., B. Maughan, P. Mortimore, J. Ouston, with A. Smith, *Fifteen Thousand Hours,* Harvard University Press, Cambridge, 1979.

Rydell, Peter, "The Economics of Early Intervention vs. Later Incarceration," in P. W. Greenwood (ed.), *The Juvenile Rehabilitation Reader,* The Rand Corporation, N-2236-OJJDP (forthcoming), 1985.

Schlossman, S., and M. Sedlak, *The Chicago Area Project Revisited,* The Rand Corporation, N-1944-NIE, 1983.

Sechrest, L., and R. Redner, "Strength and Integrity of Treatments in Evaluation Studies," in *How Well Does It Work?* National Institute of Law Enforcement and Criminal Justice, Washington, D.C., 1979.

Sechrest, L., S. O. White, and E. D. Brown (eds.), *The Rehabilitation of Criminal Offenders: Problems and Prospects,* National Academy of Sciences, Washington, D.C., 1979.

Shannon, L., *Assessing the Relationship Between Juvenile and Adult Criminal Careers,* University of Iowa, Iowa City, 1981.

Shannon, L., "A Longitudinal Study of Delinquency and Crime," in Charles Wellford, (ed.), *Quantitative Studies in Criminology,* Sage Publications, Beverly Hills, California, 1978.

Shannon, L., *The Prediction Problem as it Applies to Delinquency and Crime Control,* Department of Justice, Juvenile Justice and Delinquency Prevention, January 1983. *Science,* Vol. 199, 1978, pp. 563–564.

Shaw, C. R., and H. D. McKay, *Juvenile Delinquency and Urban Areas,* University of Chicago Press, Chicago, Illinois, 1942, Rev. ed. 1969.

Shaw, C. R., and H. D. McKay, *Social Factors in Juvenile Delinquency,* Report of the National Commission on Law Observance and Enforcement (Wickersham Commission), No. 13, Vol. 2, Washington, D.C., 1931.

Shinnar, S., and R. Shinnar, "The Effects of the Criminal Justice System on the Control of Crime: A Quantitative Approach," *Law and Society Review,* Vol. 9, No. 4, 1975, pp. 581–611.

Sutherland, E. H., and D. R. Cressey, *Principles of Criminology,* 5th Edition, Lippincott, Philadelphia, Pennsylvania, 1955.

U.S. Department of Health, Education and Welfare, *Lasting Effects After Preschool,* Washington, D.C., 1978.

U.S. Department of Justice, *Uniform Crime Report, 1982,* Washington, D.C., 1983.

Van Dusen, K., "Treatment Interventions Implied by Biological Factors," in P. W. Greenwood (ed.) *The Juvenile Rehabilitation Reader,* The Rand Corporation, N-2236-OJJDP (forthcoming), 1985.

von Hirsch, Andrew, *Doing Justice,* Hill and Wang, New York, 1976.

Walter, H. I., and S. K. Gilmore, "Placebo Versus Social Learning Affects in Parent Training Procedures Designed to Alter the Behavior of Aggressive Boys," *Behavior Therapy,* Vol. 4, 1973, pp. 361–377.

Wayson, W., and T. Lasley, "Climates for Excellence: Schools That Foster Self-Discipline," *Phi Delta Kappa,* Vol. 65, 1984.

Weber, G., *Inner City Children Can Be Taught To Read: Four Successful Schools,* Council for Basic Education, Washington, D.C., 1971.

West, D. J., and D. P. Farrington, *Who Becomes Delinquent?* Heinemann, London, 1973.

Wilson, J. Q., *"Raising Kids,"* The Atlantic Monthly, October 1983.

Wiltz, N. A., and G. R. Patterson, "An Evaluation of Parent Training Procedures Designed to Alter Inappropriate Aggressive Behavior in Boys, *Behavior Therapy,* Vol. 5, 1974, pp. 215–221.

Winick, M., "Cellular Changes During Placental and Fetal Growth," *American Journal of Obstetrics and Gynecology,* Vol. 109, 1971.

Wolfgang, M., R. M. Figlio, and T. Sellin, *Delinquency in a Birth Cohort,* University of Chicago Press, Chicago, Illinois, 1972.

Woods, M. L., *Alternatives to Imprisoning Young Offenders: Noteworthy Programs,* National Council on Crime and Delinquency, San Francisco, 1982.

Yochelson, S., and S. E. Samenow, *The Criminal Personality: A Profile for Change,* Vol. I, Jason Aronson, New York, 1976.

Yochelson, S., and S. E. Samenow, "A New Horizon for Total Change of the Criminal," in *The Criminal Personality: The Change Process,* Vol. II, Jason Aronson, New York, 1977.

Zimring, Franklin E., *The Changing Legal World of Adolescence,* Macmillan Press, New York, 1982.

Zimring, Franklin E., "Review, Juvenile Justice Standards," *Harvard Law Review,* Vol. 91, 1934 (1978).